ABOUT RAVEN GRIMASSI

Raven Grimassi is a practicing Witch and the author of several books on Wicca and Witchcraft, including the *Encyclopedia of Wicca and Witchcraft*, which was awarded Best Non-Fiction by the Coalition of Visionary Retailers in 2001, and *Wiccan Mysteries*, which was awarded Book of the Year and Best Spirtituality Book in 1998. Trained in the Family Tradition of Italian Witchcraft, Raven Grimassi is also an initiate of several Wiccan Traditions, including Britic Wicca and the Pictish-Gaelic Tradition. He is currently the Directing Elder of the Arician Ways. He has been a teacher and practitioner of Wicca and Witchcraft for over thirty years, and his former students include authors Scott Cunningham and Donald Michael Kraig. Raven is also an expert on the topic of Italian Witchcraft and is the leading authority on the works of Charles Godfrey Leland in this field. He has appeared on television and radio, is a popular lecturer at festivals and conventions across the country, and conducts a variety of workshops on magic, ritual, and personal power.

The Witch's FAMILIAR

SPIRITUAL PARTNERSHIPS FOR SUCCESSFUL MAGIC

RAVEN GRIMASSI

2003
Llewellyn Publications
St. Paul, Minnesota, 55164-0383, U.S.A.

FIRST EDITION
Second Printing, 2003

Book interior design and editing by Connie Hill
Cover design by Gavin Dayton Duffy
Moon photograph on cover © Digital Vision
"W" element in title and interior art © 2003 Eric Hotz

Library of Congress Cataloging-in-Publication Data
Grimassi, Raven
   The witch's familiar : spiritual partnerships for successful magic / Raven Grimassi.
      p. cm.
   Includes bibliographical references and index.
   ISBN 0-7387-0339-7
   1. Familiars (Spirits) 2. Magic. 3. Evocation. I. Title
BF1557.G75   2003
133.4'3—dc21   2003047448

Llewellyn Worldwide does not participate in, endorse, or have any authority or responsibility concerning private business transactions between our authors and the public.

All mail addressed to the author is forwarded but the publisher cannot, unless specifically instructed by the author, give out an address or phone number.

Any Internet references contained in this work are current at publication time, but the publisher cannot guarantee that a specific location will continue to be maintained. Please refer to the publisher's website for links to authors' websites and other sources.

The publisher recommends that readers exercise caution and common sense when contemplating the rituals and practices discussed in the text. The publisher assumes no liability for any injuries or damages caused to the reader that may result from the reader's use of content contained in this publication.

Llewellyn Publications
A Division of Llewellyn Worldwide, Ltd.
P.O. Box 64383, Dept. 0-7387-0339-7
St. Paul, MN 55164-0383, U.S.A.
www.llewellyn.com

Printed in the United States of America

In memory of Morgan,
who soars now above the meadows,
forests, hills, streams, and lakes
of the eternal Summerland

ALSO BY RAVEN GRIMASSI

Beltane

Encyclopedia of Wicca & Witchcraft

Hereditary Witchcraft

Italian Witchcraft

Wiccan Magick

The Wiccan Mysteries

The Witches' Craft

TABLE OF CONTENTS

ILLUSTRATIONS

An old magical seal for drawing the aid of good spirits.

Raven Grimassi

INTRODUCTION

This book began and ended in a very curious way—
as all things do whenever a raven is involved.
Within a few days of signing the contract to write this
book on Familiar Spirits, a young raven with a broken
wing found its way to me. I live on a ranch in the country that has so many crows and ravens visiting each day
that the place is now called Crow Haven Ranch.

Being very concerned for the well-being of the raven,
I contacted several wildlife rescue groups and discussed
the condition of the bird. In the end I was told that the
bird would have to be euthanized because its wing could
not be mended. Instead of allowing the bird to be killed,
I decided to care for it myself. Not knowing whether the
raven was a male or female, I named it Morgan, which I
felt suited either gender, but I tended to think of the bird
as "he."

The raven is my totem or power animal. I've been fas-
cinated with ravens since I was a young boy. Therefore it
was with great interest that I turned my attention to trying to gain an intimate rapport with this captive raven.
But as with the way of the raven spirit, things were not
to be as I personally envisioned.

I was initially very encouraged by Morgan's acceptance
of me within a week or two. I mused that the raven had
come to accept me much like it might accept a nearby

horse or cow in the same pasture. While always cautious, Morgan seemed neither afraid of me nor particularly interested. I continued to bring him food and water each day, and I talked to him often. By the end of the second week, I was able to gently pet Morgan across the back and down the tail feathers. To pet a wild raven and not have it attempt to flee was quite a moment for me, although I must admit that Morgan appeared to simply tolerate it rather than enjoy it.

Much to my joy, other crows and ravens came daily to visit with Morgan. One bird in particular often remained with him for about twenty to thirty minutes every day. The others seemed to come and go within a few minutes, and their primary interest appeared to be the food that Morgan had scattered outside the closure. Although Morgan would never fly again in this world, at least he was still able to enjoy the fellowship of his own kind.

As time passed, Morgan showed an interest in my comings and goings. Naturally the bird came to associate me with the appearance of food, and became noticeably excited whenever I approached the enclosure. Eventually Morgan began to make mouthing gestures in my presence, accompanied by prolonged periods of direct eye contact. I felt a bond forming that could not be described. I tried not to anthropomorphize my daily encounters with him, and I'm sure I was only moderately successful.

The greatest lesson I learned from Morgan was the lesson of the wild and the domesticated. He was a wild creature intimately attuned to the ways of surviving in Nature's daily cycle of life and death. Morgan was not a pet and would never be a pet. His instincts were always present, always sharp, and he seemed ruled by them, at least from my perspective. I believe Morgan would have argued instead that such instincts *served* him, but did not rule.

Morgan taught me that if I wanted rapport, then it was I who must adapt to ways of the wild. Morgan would only compromise so far, for his instincts for safety would always dictate the moment, the degree of contact, and the type of interaction. It was easier for me as the domesticated creature to change my behavior than it was for this creature of the wild.

The months that followed brought many unexpected events. There were times when Morgan seemed to take little notice of me and other times it was clear that he wanted some companionship. While cleaning his enclosure (a large parrot cage) one day with a garden hose, I accidentally discovered that Morgan enjoyed the equivalent of a light rain. Following this, he took to hiding food in the cracks of some old dried branches I provided for him to hop to and from. The entire enclosure lie beneath the shade of a large California peppertree, which Morgan never gave up hope of gaining access to.

The day finally arrived when this manuscript was nearing its end. One late night I turned my attention to writing the funeral rite in the last chapter. The next morning I awoke and glanced out the window only to find that I could not see Morgan in the enclosure. Morgan was always in the highest branch each morning where he could view the valley from our hilltop, as well as see the approach of winged friends and other visitors.

I rushed out to the enclosure and found Morgan's remains on the ground just a few feet inside the door. Something had killed him early that morning, and raven feathers were scattered everywhere outside of the cage. I immediately recalled the funeral ritual I had written the night before. What struck me next was the fact that nothing larger than a mouse could get into the enclosure, and Morgan's body had not been consumed. However it was clear that he had been attacked and torn apart. The latch to the door of the enclosure was a screw-down type. The door was tightly closed, and the enclosure showed no signs of being breached anywhere.

I put the mystery behind me, offered a blessing to Morgan's spirit, and then performed a rite of release. Then in accord with the Old Ways, I placed the remains on a red ant mound, with Morgan's body inside a small bird cage designed for parakeets (the distance between the bars being not quite the width of my little finger). Ants are Underworld creatures sacred to Ceres, the goddess of the Mysteries (who is also my patroness). In ancient times the bones of such creatures as toads and frogs were made available to magic users by ants using this method of cleaning.

I weighted the cage down by placing a box of Italian marble shards on top of it, so that no animals would disturb the process. I returned each day to check on the progress and by the afternoon of the second day, it was nearly completed as the bones were now entirely visible and almost entirely free of any remains. The skull, about the size of a golf ball, was the first item to be cleaned.

I returned on the morning of the third day to claim the bones for my raven shrine, only to find that once again there was no sign of Morgan. The door was still tightly latched, the cage unmoved and unbreached, no animal tracks in the loose dirt nor any signs of disturbance, and yet everything was gone. Ants do not consume bones, which is why Witches and magicians used them in this method of cleaning. However, nothing remained except for three very small, fuzzy feathers. Wherever a raven has been we can always expect a puzzle, and a troubling one at that. Ravens help us lose complacency by always challenging what we believe is our reality.

There is a factor here that needs consideration, and it has to do with Otherworld realities. Therefore it is wise to always expect the unexpected. In the pages of this book you will learn about various phenomena that may occur when you work with Familiar spirits. Summoning Familiars is not a party game or something "witchy" to do on a Saturday night. Working with Familiars is a serious business and you can fully expect to encounter occult phenomena along the way. The material in this book is designed to enable you to deal with this effectively and safely, but under no circumstances should you ever regard the protections and preparations as not being necessary, because they are. As a practitioner of the Craft for over thirty years now, please take my word for it.

In this book I have provided a series of magical seals that are designed to aid you when working with Familiars. I have also provided information to help you better understand the occult processes involved with matters related to Familiar spirits. If you faithfully follow the guidelines and instructions found in this book, you should be able to safely and effectively work with your Familiar. The ethics of working with Familiar spirits is covered in chapter two.

In the course of writing this book I created and developed a system of magical seals for the purpose of working with Familiar spirits. During the process some very interesting phenomena occurred. I attributed much of the phenomena to the fact that I was working with the concept of magical portals or doorways. The visualizations and concentration required to create the seals no doubt produced various degrees of magical energy. This energy was self-directed in a sense, even though the purpose of each seal was established as I drew out the individual symbolism.

The most profound phenomena to occur took place over a three-day period near the completion of the work. I could feel a presence moving about the house, both inside and out. Low, deep, growling sounds could be heard in various rooms of the house shortly after sunset and sometimes late into the night. This culminated in tangible "touches" on the body (usually on the back) when walking across a room. I've always regarded it as very rude when entities produce unwelcome phenomena in my home, but as an experiment I allowed this to continue for a few days.

The entity persisted in causing tangible and audible phenomena, but made no other attempts at communication. Within a
few days it became necessary to banish the entity and to close
the doorways that were opened through working with the magical concepts required to produce the seals. Through the use of
these seals you should be able to ensure control over any phenomena that might occur once you begin working with a Familiar spirit.

I created the system of magical seals for this book using time-
proven techniques and occult principles. Because I wanted this
system to be more in alignment with the Craft, I relied upon
Pagan imagery rather than the common Cabalistic images one
finds in most grimoires that have been produced since the Middle Ages. The script appearing around the seals is the Theban alphabet, an old system once very popular among Witches prior to
the 1980s. The words represented in Theban on the seals are actually Latin words. I selected them as "keywords" to indicate the
nature of each seal.

The creation of magical seals is an ancient technique of evok-
ing or invoking sources of power. The images that are employed
evoke or invoke elements of the collective subconscious/con-
scious imprints of our ancestors. What this refers to is how early
humans viewed the powers of Nature, and how they viewed life
and death. One example would be lightning striking the ground
and splitting a tree or creating a fire. To primitive people such an
act would be attributed to something supernatural, and later to a
deity. The Greek god Zeus throwing a thunder bolt is one image
of this evolved concept.

Joseph Campbell was an advocate of the theory that myths
arise from the patterns of our own biological experience of the
world around us. This is often referred to as the "firm syndrome"
of human experience. Consider that with the rising of the sun,
our primitive ancestors awoke from the night and the realm of

dreams. The night was a time of danger, and dreams often placed the dreamer in fearful situations.

The light of the sun dispelled not only darkness itself but also the fear associated with the dreamworld, and with the dangers of night in general. This served to equate light itself as a rescuer, protector, and even a messiah. Through this, human experience became patterned with the biological response to environment. This then became the format and structure for various symbols, as well as the imagery of expression related to myths and the themes they contain.

Campbell states that this reflects the unity of "the race of man" not only in its biology but also in its "spiritual history" that manifests as a "single symphony" expressed in the myths of all cultures. This is one of the reasons why I selected various symbols such as the spiral, and incorporated various images into the design of each magical seal. In effect I wanted to draw upon the commonality of human symbolism, image, and primitive imprints, which I believe are carried in genetic/ancestral memory.

In his book *The World's Rim* (University of Nebraska Press, 1967), anthropologist Hartley Burr Alexander argues for the idea that ceremony and imagery are part of the "human commonality" expressed in rituals and myths throughout the world. Alexander states that a comparison of cultural elements from distant parts of the world reveals identical patterns combined with different expressions of the one single insight. The commonality of the human experience, and of human expression, is a key ingredient in the development and structure of various symbols, as well as cultural myths and rituals.

Symbols reflect what lies behind the physical form, or within a myth, legend, or ritual. Symbols encapsulate the divine process operating behind it all, and reflect the cultural understanding of the "inner mechanism" of Nature. The symbols I selected for the magical seal designs are some of the oldest ones used by our ancestors. Used correctly they can evoke or invoke what I term "the momentum of the past."

The theory of the momentum of the past is rooted in the concept of how a catalyst begins a chain reaction. The idea here is that when something is done in the way it has always been done, century after century, a "memory association chain" is established. The connection of a concept to a symbol and the symbol's power to generate an energy response can be seen even in mundane circumstances. For example, if you're driving down a street, approaching an intersection, and you suddenly notice that the traffic light is about to turn red, there is an emotional reaction. A symbol, and the concept it represents, has instantly invoked an intense reaction within you. A memory chain association exists between you and the symbol.

The traffic light, the stop sign, and other cultural symbols are among the many symbols that have imprinted upon the minds of the people within our society. It could be argued that over many generations the "memory chain association" of a red light, a hexagon sign, and other such things could be carried within our genetic memory. This would then be passed to future generations. In time people may have an "instinctive" or intuitive response to these symbols without ever formally being taught their significance.

It is my belief that the symbols used in this book have the ability to connect one to the momentum of the past. Therefore I consider the magical seals to be effective when used in accord with time-proven methods of magical practice. Like everything in magic, the practitioner must believe in not only the system one practices but also in his or her own personal power. At the core of one's personal power is the connection between deity and the self. This is sometimes referred to as the "divine spark within."

The occult teaching indicates that we all bear within us the divine spark of that which created our souls. Just as a painting or a sculpture reflects something of the artist, or has within it some quality of the nature of the artist, so too do our souls bear the mark of the "hands" that formed them. Therefore the creative essence of the gods (the power itself to create) is part of the nature of the human soul.

Since we bear the creative spark of our creators within us, we can create, develop, and empower our own creations. The magical systems we create, and the symbols we attach to them, find their power at the very source of our link to the gods (the divine spark we bear within ourselves). This is one of the reasons magic works to begin with. I refer any reader interested in more details to my previous book, *Wiccan Magick* (Llewellyn, 1998), for further exploration of magical concepts and techniques.

It is time now to begin our journey into the world of the Familiar spirit. In the chapters that lie ahead we will explore the history of the Familiar spirit, along with the nature of Familiars and how to work with them as magical companions. Spells, rites, and other things related to working with Familiars await in the pages of this book. Let us begin our quest.

1

HISTORY

OF THE

FAMILIAR SPIRIT

I n this chapter we will explore the occult concept of the Familiar spirit in Witchcraft.
According to ancient lore, a spirit from the Otherworld was believed able to dwell within the
physical body of an animal or creature. The traditional vessels for such spirits were the cat, mouse,
ferret, hare, bat, snake, hound, or bird—particularly a raven or an owl. The lore surrounding the
Familiar spirit indicates that a Witch received
one following initiation into the Witches' sect.

A magical connection between humans and
animals has its roots in Paleolithic and Neolithic
concepts, and is evident in old shamanic
practices associated with animal guides. Various
drawings and etchings in cave art depict ritual-
ized scenes that are believed to represent magical
themes. A variety of artifacts from these periods
represent different animals and creatures carved

and painted by ancient artisans. Many of these identical creatures later appear as Familiar spirits in the lore of Witchcraft. This is highly suggestive of a survival theme related to ancient beliefs and practices.

In the earliest writings about Witches the creatures associated with Witchcraft all possess a chthonic nature. We find many of them to be creatures of woodlands, wetlands, and caves. This association links them to Underworld themes and to Underworld deities such as Hecate, Diana, Proserpina, Morrigan, Macha, Badb, and Nemain. To our ancestors, the night and the moon were intimately linked to the Otherworld or Spirit World. Folk beliefs held that in the night many supernatural beings inhabited the dark and wooded places.

The Concept of a Familiar

The basic concept of a Familiar spirit most likely arose from a human need to communicate with the unseen world of spirits. At first the Familiar spirit served as a type of mediator between the worlds. Later, the concept of a companion and ally evolved. As we shall see later in this chapter, with the rise of Christianity the Church viewed the Familiar spirit as a servant given to the Witch by the Devil of Judeo-Christian religion. In this biased and distorted view of the Familiar spirit the creature was portrayed as a "partner in evil" who aided the Witch in casting harmful spells.

As humankind became civilized, establishing farms, cities, and the supporting structures associated with such communities, a resulting loss of connection with Nature occurred. Instead of working in a "common cause" with Nature, humans set about trying to master Nature. All of Nature came to be viewed as a resource for the gain of humankind. In response, the spirits of Nature withdrew from the company of humans.

By contrast the Witch seeks to maintain rapport with Nature and to live his or her life in partnership. Wild animals, and some "domesticated" animals such as the cat, are more in tune with Nature in daily life than are the vast majority of human beings. Establishing communication with such animals brings one closer to the source to which these creatures themselves are attuned. Possessing a Familiar spirit allows the Witch to merge with the instincts of the animal and thereby interface with the *intelligence* of Nature.

The physical senses such as hearing and smell are more acute in animals than in human beings. From an occult perspective, the psychic senses of animals are stronger as well. A close rapport with the Familiar spirit enhances the psychic abilities of the Witch. The Familiar also benefits from having a relationship with the Witch. Merging with human consciousness provides the Familiar with an expanded view of reality, and intensifies the energy pattern of the Familiar. The alien worlds of human consciousness and "natural order" consciousness join together to form a magical consciousness. In this the Familiar becomes the mediator.

The magical consciousness of the Witch and the Familiar can open portals to other realms, and can accomplish works of magic in the material realm as well as the astral plane. This is the basis of legends in which we find the magical servant of the Witch, and tales of shapeshifting by Witches. In reality the Familiar is a magical partner and companion for the Witch, and vice versa.

The oldest concept of the Witches' Familiar was the spirit-animal belonging to the group consciousness of a specific type of animal. In other words, this was the spirit of the entire species delimited into a single form. In some cultures this is called a power animal or animal guide. Such an entity can be used as a doorway or link connecting to the higher animal spirit or nature.

In such cases the astral form of the animal becomes the vehicle for working with the greater consciousness.

The concept of the Witches' Familiar is connected with shamanic practices and the lore of magical creatures from many cultures. One of the earliest and most clear signs of the relationship between humans and guardian animal spirits is reflected in the *Ver Sacrum*, the ancient Italic rite of the Sacred Springtime predating the rise of the Roman Empire. Every spring season ancient Italic tribes observed a custom wherein a portion of the tribe was required to divide off and form new colonies. Their sacred animal guided each tribe in this endeavor, leading them to new lands in which to establish villages. The people known as the Sabellians were guided by a bull, the Piceni by a woodpecker, the Lucani by a wolf, and so forth.

Many of the animals associated with various deities, such as Diana and the hound, Hecate and the toad, Proserpina and the serpent, Pan and the goat, are animals that also appear as Witches' Familiars in the vast literature on Witchcraft. It is worthy of note to realize that the various types of Familiars mentioned in Witch trials are the same creatures associated with moon goddesses, mother goddesses, and ancient chthonic deities. In particular these are the frog/toad, snake, bird, and lizard among many others. This is an indication of the antiquity of pre-Christian themes found in Witchcraft, and demonstrates a longstanding mystical tradition.

Over the course of time humans personified various spirits and the forces of Nature. The concept of fairies and other supernatural beings blended together into a common mythos. Historian Jeffrey Burton Russell, in his book *Witchcraft in the Middle Ages* (London: Cornell University, 1972), writes, "The small demons that became the Witches' Familiars of the later Middle Ages were originally dwarves, trolls, fairies, elves, kobolds, or the fertility spirits called Green Men. . . ." He adds that black and green were the favored colors of Witches, and that green was a fairy color. Historian Diane Purkiss (*The Witch in History*, London: Routledge, 1996) comments on Familiars as being malevolent fairies. Viewing Familiars as remnants of earlier pagan spirits suggests a survival theme of pre-Christian religion within the folklore and folk magic traditions associated with Witchcraft of the Middle Ages and early Renaissance periods.

Richard Baxter (1615–1619) was an earlier figure who viewed Familiars as Nature spirits. Baxter was a Puritan cleric who wrote a treatise titled *The Certainty of the World of Spirits*, which was published in the year of his death. The treatise argued for the belief in "invisible powers and spirits." Baxter believed that such things aided Witches in raising storms and casting spells. In his treatise Baxter wrote that it is uncertain whether the spirits that served Witches "are neither Angels, good or bad" or "whether those called Fairies and Goblins are not such." The fact that the latter concept was even a consideration here demonstrates the survival of such Pagan beliefs into later periods.

Nonphysical Familiars

One of the persistent themes in the literature of Witchcraft is the tale of Witches being transported to the Sabbat through the aid of a Familiar spirit. In Fairy lore there are also many accounts of humans being transported into the Fairy Realm. This is suggestive of an Otherworld experience, a crossing between the realms of mortals and spirits by the intervention of a supernatural being. According to oral tradition, in order to avoid detection some Witches met within the astral realm to hold their Sabbats. This often included the use of "flying ointment" smeared upon the skin. In Fairy lore either a magical dust or a potion is used.

According to the literature on Witchcraft, the Witches' flying ointment was made from herbs: aconite (wolfsbane), belladonna, hemlock, smallage, and cinquefoil. This was mixed with a paste made from the meal of fine wheat, or with fat or oil. In order to be nonlethal, such a recipe would have to be concocted under the guidance of a master herbalist, as even small amounts of some of these herbs are deadly. We know that the earliest word for Witch in Western literature was the Greek word *pharmakis*, which means one who possesses the knowledge of herbs.

Inducing a trance, whether through meditation, chemicals, or other means, can link the Witch to other realms of existence and to altered states of consciousness. One ancient technique involved listening to the croaking of frogs as an aid to entering a trance. Here we see the connection of the animal spirit as a magical partner to the Witch figure. The fact that the frog moves back and forth between land and water perhaps suggested a supernatural power to lead the Witch to and from the spirit realm. Nineteenth-century folklorists such as Charles Leland, Roma Lister, and J. B. Andrews noted the incorporation of small bronze frog images used by Witches for spells and other works of magic, which seems to indicate a magical connection and relationship between frogs and Witches.

From an occult perspective, trance (as an altered state of consciousness) is conducive to astral projection, which allows the consciousness to leave the physical body and travel as desired. Astral projection is a theme that appears in the literature on Witchcraft even as late as the seventeenth century, where it is called "traveling in spirit" or "journeying without the body." Such tales appearing in Witch trial transcripts are consistent throughout Europe.

In some writings a Witch's Familiar is a fairy or imp. Such creatures are said to dwell in spirit realms, and doorways from this world lead into the Otherworld. Traveling "in spirit" allowed the Witch to enter the Otherworld that exists beyond the physical world. Perhaps this is why the fairy and the Witch are often associated in folk beliefs throughout much of Europe and the British Isles.

The Church and the Familiar Spirit

In 1318 Pope John XXII sent nine alleged Witches to be prosecuted for various magical practices, including contacting Familiar spirits with the aid of a polished glass. The Church employed several scriptures from the Old Testament concerning Familiar spirits, although it is unclear what the concept would have meant to ancient Hebrews in comparison to the Christian Church of the Middles Ages and Renaissance periods. Many have used the story of the "Witch of Endor" from the Old Testament (1 Samuel 28: 3–25) as a foundation stone concerning the Church's view on Familiars. However, there is nothing in the original language to indicate that the woman in question was a Witch. Here she is referred to as a *ba'alath ob*, literally a "mistress of the Ob." The Latin translation read *mulierem habentem pythonem*, which means "a woman possessing an oracle spirit." It is the King James version that translated the later Latin rendering to mean "possessing a Familiar spirit."

Sorcerers or necromancers who evoked the dead to answer questions were referred to in Hebrew as an *ob*. Some commentators have suggested that "ob" refers to a leather bottle, and therefore this nickname arose from the belief that a sorcerer's body could serve as a vessel for a spirit from the Otherworld. Such commentators claim that the Greek word *pytho* was used in much the same regard to denote both the person and the spirit within the sorcerer. However, historian Frederick H. Ceyer, in his article "Magic in Ancient Syria-Palestine—and in the Old Testament" (appearing in the book *Witchcraft and Magic in Europe: Biblical and Pagan Societies*, Ankarloo and Stuart, University of Pennsylvania Press, 2001) states that the precise meaning of ob eludes us.

The King James Bible rendered the translation to read "Familiaris." This changed the meaning of the original scripture, and now indicated a "household servant." This was done in order to portray such spirits as being the personal servants of a sorcerer. The literal translations of the Bible do not actually address the Familiar spirit; biblical scripture deals mainly with practitioners of the occult arts. The Book of Deuteronomy 18:10–11 admonished one not to keep company with any who is a fortuneteller, soothsayer, charmer, diviner, spell-caster, a spirit medium, or anyone who seeks oracles from the dead. The Book of Leviticus 20:27 called for a strict penalty: "A man or a woman who acts as a medium or fortuneteller shall be put to death by stoning." The King James Bible replaced the original concept and inserted the word "witch."

The Court and the Familiar Spirit

In the year 1563, Queen Elizabeth issued a Witchcraft statute that decreed a penalty for anyone who invoked or conjured "evil and wicked Spirites." A later statute introduced by King James in 1604 was more specific:

> That if any person or persons . . . shall use practise or exercise any Invocation or Conjuration of any evil and wicked Spirit, or shall consult covenant with entertaine employ feede or rewarde any evil and wicked Spirit (they will be punished).*

Local court officials anxious to convict people of Witchcraft used coercion to shape the evidence in such a way that suspected Witches were in clear violation of the law (i.e., feeding or entertaining evil spirits).

An interesting theme that appears in Witch trial transcripts is the mention of the inherited Familiar. Most scholars view the

---

* Used with permission, © Thomas Donaldson, 1995.

Familiar spirit as primarily part of English Witchcraft, although it appears in the Witch trial transcripts of other regions of Europe as well. One example is the Venetian trial of Elena Draga and Maddalena la Greca, who claimed to possess a *fada* in the form of a chicken. A fada is a fairy-like creature, and in modern Italian is called a *fata*. The Familiar spirit also appears in the Salem Witchcraft trials in New England.

In the Chelmsford trial (1556), the accused confessed to possessing a white-spotted cat named Sathan that was passed down from Witch to Witch. In another Chelmsford trial (1582), a twelve-year-old girl named Elizabeth Frauncis said she received a cat from her grandmother, but later gave it away to a woman named Agnes Waterhouse. In a trial held at St. Osyth (1582), Margerie Sammon claimed she had inherited her Familiars.

English Witch trials contained accounts of suspected Witches having relationships with animal Familiars. The main period of such focus was between 1550–1650. Matthew Hopkins, the infamous "Witch Finder General," used the possession of a Familiar spirit as the primary criterion for proving a person guilty of practicing Witchcraft. As a result many people were executed on the grounds that they kept animals or had a strange mark on their body, said to be the nipple used to feed the Familiar.

Thomas A. Donaldson, in his 1995 essay "The Role of the Familiar in English Witch Trials" (http://home.earthlink.net/~tad5/familiar.html), defines Familiars as "first and foremost, spirits." He states that:

> These spirits usually had their own names, communicated to human beings through speech, and sometimes displayed distinct personalities and motives. Most of these spirits took on the physical form of a domestic animal and established a relationship with a particular person, often a woman with evil intentions. They helped the "Witch" carry out her maleficia; in this respect the

trial records depict them as having incredible, unearthly powers. The Familiar was by no means a subservient, faithful helper who followed the Witch's every command. The relationship between the Familiar and the Witch is better characterized as "give-and-take." Some Familiars played the role of little devils in that they requested a pact (often satanic in nature) before they would perform any services for the Witch. Furthermore, almost all of them craved nourishment in the form of human blood. They would attach themselves to some part of the Witch's body and suck blood out of her, leaving a bruise that Witch hunters called the "Witch's mark." The Familiars and Witch's mark acted as a strong evidence in the many trials.*

The trials held in Chelmsford, St. Osyth, Warboys, and Lancaster found a combined total of forty-six individuals guilty of practicing Witchcraft in connection with a Familiar spirit. Donaldson notes that the courts readily exchanged the term "Familiar spirit" with other words such "imp," "devil," or "demon." Therefore it is not surprising that the oldest concept of the Familiar spirit mutated under the direction of secular and ecclesiastical authority.

The courts extracted "evidence" that the Familiar typically initiated contact with the Witch. Once attached to the Witch, it appeared that he or she rarely had any choice but to keep it. Another interesting element that appears in trial transcripts is the account of each Familiar arriving with its own name already established. In other words, reportedly the Witch did not name the Familiar. Matthew Hopkins remarked that "no mortall could invent" such names, which suggested to him something diabolical. Donaldson states that the fact animal Familiars had their own pre-existing names fits with what is known of the general magi-

---

* Donaldson. Ibid.

cal beliefs in this time period. People of this era commonly believed that all spirits possessed names, and therefore it only made sense that Familiars had their own unique names.

Once established with the Witch, the Familiar served a variety of functions. Trial records reflect that Familiars inflicted injury or caused death to both humans and animals. Haunting or generally harassing people was also accredited to the Witches' Familiar. In general this was limited to verbal assault, jeering, or threatening the targeted person. Perhaps some powerless individuals of this era fantasized the service of a spirit to vent their rage and anger at some real or imagined sense of oppression. No doubt there were some Witches who did invoke their Familiars to carry out magical attacks against their enemies.

Donaldson points out that when examining trial transcripts it is difficult to tell whether the Witch or the Familiar is the one in charge. It appears in most recorded accounts that Familiars often did perform services for the Witches. The relationship was not necessarily one of "mistress and servant" but involved a give-and-take relationship. Each party had something to gain in the relationship. In some trials a formal pact or binding agreement between the Witch and the Familiar was required.

The Familiar sought nourishment from the Witch in either blood or breast milk. Witches reportedly sometimes fed milk and bread to their Familiars, but the Familiar craved human blood. Occult theories of the period suggested that the Familiar required blood in order for it to maintain a corporal body, since it was actually a spirit. According to trial records the Familiars obtained blood from the Witch by pricking a place on his or her body and sucking out the blood. This left a mark on the body that was identified by Witch hunters as the "Witch's mark" or the "Devil's mark."

In reality any mark, bruise, mole, or abnormality of the skin was enough to convince the Witch hunters that they had exposed a Witch. Commonly, with aging, the skin develops dark spots, moles, and other growths, and most accused individuals were elderly. To counter this, Witch hunters maintained that a Witch's mark is usually found in "an unusual place" like the tailbone or genital region. Witch marks were said to be insensible to pain caused by a pin or a needle thrust into them.

Donaldson notes a commentary on the Lancaster trial written by G. B. Harrison in 1929. In the article Harrison proposes that Familiars were not spirits but simply Witches in animal disguise:

> But the spirits which appear now as men, now as animals, are, at first sight, more difficult to explain until it is remembered that in the Witchcraft ritual the members of the coven disguise themselves as animals . . . [the Familiars] are nothing more than the evil humans who were responsible for the whole business.*

The Modern Witch and the Familiar

Most modern Witches have their own unique view of what constitutes a Familiar spirit. No contemporary Witches accept the Judeo-Christian view of the Familiar as accurate or valid. Many modern Witches tend to perceive the Familiar in much the same way that some American Indian traditions view animal guides or power animals. In this regard they are messengers to and from the Otherworld and are gifted to one by the Great Spirit. They are also healers and powerful allies for those with whom they form a relationship.

For the modern Witch there are essentially three types of Familiar spirit: the physical, the astral/spirit, and the artificial Familiar. The physical Familiar can be a pet or any animal/creature

---

* Donaldson. Ibid.

to which you feel drawn. The astral/spirit Familiar is one that pre-exists as a conscious entity within the elemental realm or the Otherworld, which lies beyond the world of the living. The artificial Familiar is one that can be created through magic.

Familiars can assist the Witch in carrying energy for healing, communication, or spell casting. The Familiar can also be used for protection of the home and/or personal property. During sessions of astral projection or dream work the Familiar can safeguard the Witch on many levels. The Familiar can also retrieve information on the planes, both inner and outer. These aspects are covered in the chapters that follow.

Let us turn now to the next chapter and explore how one obtains a Familiar, and the nature of the Familiar spirit.

Notice To Reader

In the following chapter appear the concepts of "binding" and "controlling" familiar spirits. Please note that these are old traditional magical terms and have been used here in keeping with the style of an antique Grimoire. For the purposes of this book the term binding refers to "connecting" or "housing" in order to provide a physical base from which to operate. It does not mean to imprison or hold captive. The term "control" is used to indicate "directing" and is not intended to suggest domination against personal will.

2

CHOOSING YOUR
FAMILIAR

At some point during your journey down the
path of Witchcraft you may wish the companionship of a Familiar spirit (see chapter five
for precautions). The selection of a Familiar spirit
is a personal matter. In some cases, however, the
Familiar might pick the Witch instead. Two of
the most common methods of acquiring a Familiar are "natural affinity" and the "journey quest."

If you feel naturally attracted to an animal or
creature, then it is likely that you are being called
into a relationship. During the years of practicing
Witchcraft you will probably acquire more than
one Familiar in this way. Some Witches prefer to
seek out their Familiar spirit through a guided
meditation known as a journey quest. The quest
incorporates occult symbolism into a series of visualized actions.

Before performing the actual guided meditation in the following section, it is very important

that you first read the entire book. This will help you understand exactly what it is you're doing, what to expect, and how to safely work with Familiars. Read the following preparations at this time, and make the recording suggested in the "Journey Quest" section. Upon completion of the book you can then perform the meditation if that is your choice. It is important to then re-read part one and part two in this chapter before actually performing the meditation through which you will acquire your Familiar.

In appendix two I have presented the classic Familiars that appeared in Witchcraft trials. I have included this material for a variety of purposes. One reason is to acquaint the reader with the lore associated with Familiars, and another is to plant a seed in the mind for the guided meditation. Since archaic elements of the relationship between "animal guide" and Witch are reflected in the distorted trial accounts regarding Familiars, it is helpful to possess knowledge of the pre-Christian elements. I recommend reading the appendix to better understand the archaic elements of the Familiar prior to working with one.

Part One:
The Journey Quest

I will now introduce you to the quest for your Familiar spirit. At the outset of your journey, you will not know what your Familiar may be once you encounter it. The first thing that you must do is to alter your consciousness. If you know how to meditate deeply, then this will do nicely. If not, you will need something to induce a trance-like state. This can be accomplished with the aid of a slow strobe light, or a steady slow drumbeat. You may wish to aid this with an alcoholic drink (or some other substance) in moderation. If performing the quest alone, set an alarm clock to ring in one hour, and put the clock close by.

Next you will need either a tape recorder or a friend to read the following mental journey to you. Before you begin, you will need to locate a cave or some other opening into the earth in your area. If you cannot, then you can substitute a painting or poster that contains a cave. This opening is going to be your visualization point of entrance and exit. A cave near Lake Nemi, in Italy, served this purpose for hundreds of years. In fact, a legend emerged claiming this particular cave was the entrance to the Underworld of the gods.

Listen to the audio tape of this script, or your friend reading it out loud, as you meditate upon the imagery as described. The reading should be done slowly, in a soft monotone style. Pause briefly where space is indicated by three periods, and a little longer where six periods appear. This will allow time for deeper visualization. All you need at this stage is a power stone—a quartz crystal is best. When you are ready, hold it in your left hand. The script is as follows:

> Sit comfortably and close your eyes. Take in a deep breath . . . hold it . . . and let it out. Again, take in a deep breath . . . hold it . . . and let it out. One last time, take in a deep breath . . . hold it . . . and let it out. You're feeling lighter . . . and you feel yourself gently floating up . . . up and away . . . out of this place and time.
>
> Now you're drifting . . . you're passing over buildings . . . . . . you're passing over fields . . . . . . you can see this all below you . . . . . . you're moving off into the distance.
>
> Below you is a meadow . . . and you begin to feel yourself becoming heavier . . . . . . now you begin to gently descend . . . down . . . getting lower . . . down . . . and now you're softly landing on the ground in the meadow.

You see before you, in the distance, a large hill . . . . . .
and you rise and walk toward it . . . . . . you can see
that the hill is covered with deep green moss . . . . . .
you continue to walk toward the hill . . . . . . now you
can see an opening in the hill, it is a cave.

The opening to the cave is large and round. You can
see that the entrance goes deep . . . but you cannot see
the back of the tunnel wall . . . now you begin to notice that the cave is dimly lighted by a magical glow
coming from the walls . . . . . . and you can make out
the path into the cave.

You begin to walk into the tunnel . . . . . . you can feel
the walls of the cave all around you . . . . . . as you
continue to walk, you notice that the tunnel begins to
turn to the left . . . . . . you follow it as it curves . . .

You continue to walk deeper, and deeper, into the
cave. Now you notice that the tunnel ends a few feet
in front of you . . . you walk up to the wall and touch
it with your hand. You realize that the wall is not solid
. . . . . . and so you step forward and pass through it . . .

You are now in a small clearing within a forest . . . you
appear to somehow be outside even though you are
inside . . . . . . the clearing is magically lighted, and the
place is peaceful . . . in the center you see a deep pool
of water . . . . . . beside it is a rock, large enough to sit
upon . . . . . . you sit on the rock and look around.

You are surrounded by the thickness of trees all
around . . . . . . and behind the trees there is only darkness . . . . . . and now you hear a stirring in the woods
. . . . . . a rustling sound moves toward you in the trees.

From out of the thickness of the trees in front of you, something emerges from the trees . . . . . . you sit quietly and look at it . . . . . . now it begins to move toward you in a friendly manner . . . . . . it draws nearer . . . and now is only a few feet away . . . and it comes to a rest.

You extend your left hand outward, palm facing up. Suddenly a stone appears in your hand, bearing a symbol on its surface . . . you look at the symbol . . . . . . and now you look back at the creature in front of you.

You ask the creature what its name is, and you listen for a reply . . . . . . now the creature looks over at the pool of water . . . and you turn and look behind you into the water . . . . . .

You look back at the creature, and it begins to leave now . . . you watch it withdraw back into the trees . . . back into the darkness . . . . . . and now it is gone from sight.

It is time now to leave this place . . . time to return . . . and so you rise and walk back over to the wall through which you entered this place . . . . . . you find again that the wall is not solid, and so you pass through it, and back into the cave again.

You begin to follow the tunnel out of the cave . . . walking back along the path . . . . . . and now you notice that the tunnel begins to turn to the right . . . . . . you continue to move through the tunnel . . . you can feel the walls around you . . . and you continue back toward the entrance.

You can see light up ahead . . . it is the opening of the cave . . . and you move toward it . . . getting closer . . . and now you pass through the opening and back into the field outside.

You walk now back across the meadow . . . back to where you first landed . . . . . . and now you come to the spot . . . and you sit down. Take in a deep breath . . . hold it . . . and let it out. Again, take in a deep breath . . . hold it . . . and let it out. One last time, take in a deep breath . . . hold it . . . and let it out.

You're feeling lighter . . . and you feel yourself gently floating up . . . up and away . . . out of this place and time.

Now you're drifting . . . you're passing over fields . . . . . . you're passing over buildings . . . . . . you can see this all below you . . . . . . you're moving off into the distance.

Below you is the familiar setting from which you began this journey . . . and you begin to feel yourself becoming heavier . . . . . . now you begin to gently de-scend . . . down . . . getting lower . . . down . . . and now you're softly landing on the ground.

Take in a deep breath . . . hold it . . . and let it out. Again, take in a deep breath . . . hold it . . . and let it out. One last time, take in a deep breath . . . hold it . . . and let it out. Become aware of the surface beneath you, feel it, and rock back and forth a little. Place your palms on the ground, press down, and feel the physi-cal presence . . . you have now returned to the pres-ent, to this time and place from which you started.

Once you have completed this exercise it is important that you have something to drink and at least a small snack. This will help ground you and normalize your senses.

Having successfully completed this technique you have now met your Familiar. In the unlikely event that this does not occur, try it again on another day and make sure there are no distractions. The image that the familiar presented to you in creature form during the journey is deeply connected to your inner self in some special and significant way. You may like the creature that presented itself to you, and you may not. This is not important for now, so do not dwell upon it or fret about it. You may or may not, have received a name from your Familiar. If not, see "Naming the Familiar" in chapter three.

Some people will say that what you encountered was the "collective conscious" of that entity's life form. Others may say it was a "Nature spirit," or an "elemental," or perhaps even an isolated extension of your own consciousness. The only definition that matters, however, is your own. Whatever you choose to rationalize it with, the fact remains that it is your Familiar Spirit. There are many excellent books to consult on a variety of animal forms, and you can obtain more information on your Familiar. I have added a suggested reading section in the back of this book to further help you.

Part Two:
Creating the Links

This section applies to nonphysical Familiars only. Once you have discovered what your Familiar spirit is, it is then time to create the links that will maintain control over the Familiar should such a need arise. This requires the construction of a seal designed to sigilize the Familiar. A sigil differs from a symbol in that a symbol represents something, whereas a sigil is the thing itself from a magical perspective. For the purposes of this book, you can use a piece of parchment or a small, soft clay disk to serve as your seal.

It is a very old occult belief that knowing a name gives one power over the associated person or creature. Therefore, you will need to transform the name of your Familiar into a sigil. To accomplish this, write the name out on a piece of paper near the top of the page. Cross out any letters that are repeated in the name, and then write the remaining letters in order of appearance below the original name.

The next phase is to combine the remaining letters together to form a design. You can overlap the letters, place them back to back, upside-down, or in any arrangement that pleases you (as long as each letter touches one or more of the other letters). What you want to accomplish is the formation of a design that no longer looks like recognizable letters or a name. Experiment with the design until you find one that feels right to you. Try to keep the design as simple as possible.

Once you have the design, then make a drawing of the Familiar animal form, or cut and paste from clip art. Size the image to fit in the direct center sphere of the Genesis Seal (see fig. 1, p. 29). You can photocopy the seal on parchment paper, sizing it as desired, or you can redraw it, or even etch it into soft clay. Beneath the image (and within the inner sphere) you will inscribe the sigil you created from the Familiar's name. If you have something associated with the animal such as a feather, piece of fur, claw, and so forth, you can then attach it to the outer edge of the seal with glue.

Now that you have constructed the Genesis Seal, you will need to charge it with magical energy. Begin the process when the moon is in the sign of Cancer, Scorpio, or Pisces by preparing an incense made of cedar, sandalwood, and juniper. Pour out some sea salt, making a triangle large enough to surround the incense burner. Place a pure white candle outside of the triangle at each tip (anoint each candle with an oil blend of cedar, sandalwood, and juniper).

On the night of the full moon pour a cup of water into a clear glass and set it out beneath the moon. Let the moonlight fall upon it for a few moments, and then place the palm of your left hand a few inches above the cup. Extend your right hand up to the moon, palm facing it, and form a V-like shape by stretching your index finger and thumb away from each other. Fold the other three fingers inward. Then move your left hand in a clockwise circular motion above the cup, and recite these words:

> *By the Lady—*
> *May moonlight fall upon this glass,*
> *And thus into water thy magic pass.*

This is now your charged moon water. Put it in a sealed container and store it away, keeping it out of direct sunlight.

On the night of the following new moon, pour a cup of whole milk into a pan and heat it so that it will boil. Add nine drops of the charged moon water. Next add a drop of your blood taken from a finger prick, or some body fluid produced by genital stimulation, in order to create a "life-giving" connection between you and the milk. While the milk is heating to a boil, place the completed seal on your work area, and below this set an egg in a small bowl. When the milk is near boiling, break the egg open in the bowl, look at the seal and say:

> *Born to me this night, this hour,*
> *In sigil, form, and will's desire.*
> *What becomes of this, becomes of you,*
> *To be, or not, by magic true.*

When the milk is boiling, suspend the seal over the pot so that the seal is essentially in the steam. Then, looking at the seal, say:

> *Suckled, nurtured, on this day you are born,*
> *Your spirit now resides in this magical form.*
> *You and the seal, now one to be,*
> *Bound or released, as so willed by me.*

When not in use, take the seal and wrap it in a piece of silk. Silk protects an object from releasing energy or randomly drawing surrounding energy to it. Keep the seal in a safe place away from direct sunlight. The seal is, magically speaking, the life-force connection of "soul to body" for the astral/spirit Familiar. It gives you a degree of control over the Familiar and allows you to sever the Familiars connection to the material plane should you need to do so. Breaking the connection will normally cause the Familiar to withdraw back into the astral/spirit realm within a few short days. The technique for severing connections is covered in chapter five.

As a precautionary measure you will now charge a pencil that has an eraser. The technique for using the pencil when needed is provided in part three of this chapter. Take the pencil and anoint it on the middle section with the egg and the milk, using only a tiny drop. Take a strip of silk, dip it in the moon water, and then wrap it around the anointed area of the pencil, sealing the charge in place. You may want to tape or tie the strip in order to secure it to the pencil. Then, hold the pencil in your right hand, and looking at it say these words:

> *Spirit to spirit, flesh to flesh warm,*
> *The power resides here now to give form.*
> *All drawn with this tool then becomes real,*
> *And is bound and transformed under magical seal.*

Once the Genesis Seal has been completed along with the charged pencil, it is time then to create a version of the Witches' Ladder. The purpose of this ladder is to bind magical charges into a series of nine knots tied in a cord. These magical charges will be used later to charge the nine seals that appear in this book.

Take a cord that is eighteen inches in length, anoint the ends with a small drop of moon water, and then wrap it into a coil. Making sure no water will stain the Genesis Seal, set the coiled cord directly upon it. Next place the pencil on the cord, arranging it horizontally in front of you. To charge the cord, place the palm of your left hand a few inches above the cord, and visualize the cord enveloped in a sphere of energy generated by the seal and the charged pencil. Then, looking at the cord, say these words:

> *Between the worlds, here in this space,*
> *Upon thee now this spell I place.*
> *Receive from two all in accord,*
> *So be it done here by my word.*

Now pick up the cord, and prepare to tie nine knots in it. Before tying each individual knot, say the following words each time, ending by firmly drawing the knot tight in the cord as you speak the last word:

> *With this knot I here do bind,*
> *Like unto like, each to its kind.*
> *Untied, the power flows great with zeal,*
> *Empowering and charging each magical seal.*

Now put the cord away in a closed box or cabinet, along with the seal and the pencil. Keep these items out of direct sunlight as exposure will cause some of the energy to dissipate.

Using the Magical Cord

To charge and awaken any one of the nine seals described in section three, burn an incense of cedar, sandalwood, and juniper. Suspend the seal from a string directly at eye level. Use a piece of tape to adhere the back of the seal to the thread. Next hold the cord up to the seal and touch the knot to the seal. Then, untie a knot as you look directly at the design on the talisman seal. When the knot is untied bring your hands together so that the cord goes limp and sags. Next, move the cord toward the seal, and then quickly pull the cord tight so that it "snaps" against the seal. Time the snap to occur as you say the very last word of the following incantation:

> At this time, and in this hour,
> Pass I now to thee the power!

Repeat this technique for each of the seals when they are needed. Remember to keep the cord put away when not in use. Once the last of the nine knots has been untied, you can dispose if it by burning it to ashes. The remains should then be buried in soil.

Part Three:
Controlling the Familiar

There may come a time when you will have to take active control over a Familiar. This is not unlike having to deal with an unruly child who demonstrates inappropriate or unacceptable behavior. Familiars are sentient beings, a fact that must always be kept in mind. In the early stages of the relationship the Familiar is dependent upon the human companion, and tends to want to please. As time passes, the Familiar may demonstrate a more independent nature and may not comply as readily with requests as in the beginning. In very rare cases the Familiar can become defiant and entirely self-directed. This must be corrected immediately.

To exercise control over the Familiar will require the use of one of the magical seals in this book. The first seal to use is the seal to control an errant Familiar. This one will usually restore compliance and restore things to the original friendly state. If this should not produce the expected results then you will have to resort to the Genesis Seal and make corrective changes.

In effect, the Genesis Seal is to the Familiar as the human body is to the soul. Altering the physical nature of the seal will create the corresponding astral counterpart to manifest in the spirit-double of the Familiar. This is where the pencil becomes a tool, for you can add something to the Familiar image on the seal. One example would be a leash or chain in order to provide some leverage for control. Another idea would be to draw a cage around the Familiar. The additions can later be erased to remove the effect. When the time comes to dissolve the Familiar's connection to the material realm, the seal can be deactivated (see chapter five).

For the purposes of this book I have included nine seals in addition to the Genesis Seal, and the Vortex Seal. There are three ways of creating the seals for personal use. The best method is to draw the seals on parchment using magical ink such as Dragon's Blood or Bat's Blood. These inks are not made from animals, and most occult/witch shops carry them. The easiest method for creating seals is to photocopy the images onto parchment or some special paper. The alternative method is to photocopy the seals and then trace over them with a wand or athame, visualizing energy flowing from you into the design.

Drawing the seals yourself by hand infuses some of your personal power into the seal. This is because it requires more concentration and focus, and therefore establishes a stronger magical connection. If you feel that you do not possess the artistic ability, you can make a photocopy and trace over the image with a charcoal pencil. Then lay the charcoal drawing facedown on the parchment and make a "rubbing" by running a small block of wood back and forth firmly across the blank side of the photocopy. This will transfer the image to the parchment. Then you can use a pen to give the transfer better detail. Add the words on the seal afterward, as using the charcoal tracing will reverse the letters. Now let's look at each of the seals and their unique nature.

The Genesis Seal

The purpose of the Genesis Seal is to create a magical link that sustains the Familiar within the material dimension. The Genesis Seal features a serpent swallowing its tail, which is the symbol of the cycle of rebirth. Three spirals appear around the serpent, symbolizing the power of transformation. The number three represent the forces that bring about manifestation: time, place, and energy.

A series of words of power are inscribed in the Witches' alphabet and encircle the seal. The spoken words of invocation for this seal are:

> *Suckled, nurtured, on this day you are born,*
> *Your spirit now resides in this magical form.*
> *You and the seal, now one to be,*
> *Bound or released, as so willed by me.*

Fig. 1: The Genesis Seal

The Seal of Calling

The purpose of this seal is to evoke/invoke or summon your Familiar whenever you have need of it. The Seal of Calling features the mystical hand of divinity appearing from a cloud. The cloud represents manifestation of spiritual forces in the magical ether. Three spirals appear at the command of the divine hand, for three is the mystical number of manifestation. The spirals represent portals to and from the Otherworld. The hand appears in the gesture of reaching for a door, and thereby signals the opening of the magical portal.

A series of words of power are inscribed in the Witches' alphabet and encircle the seal. Each word is separated by a star, which symbolizes the astral forces at work. The spoken words of invocation for this seal are:

> (Familiar's name), *thee I call by moon and tide,*
> *From height and depth, both far and wide.*

Fig. 2: The Seal of Calling

The Seal of Departing

The purpose of this seal is to send your Familiar back to its natural realm, or to give it release from the material plane. The Seal
of Departing features the entrance to a cave. Since ancient times
caves have been entrances to the Underworld. Depicted among
the rocks appear three spirals, which symbolize transformation.
Three is the mystical number of manifestation. Marking the four
quarters of north, east, south, and west appear ancient chevron
symbols, which symbolizes the pubic/vulva area, or birth and regeneration.

A series of words of power inscribed in the Witches' alphabet
encircles the seal. Each word is separated by a star, symbolizing
the astral forces at work. The spoken words of invocation for this
seal are:

> (Familiar's name), *go thee now and take thy*
> *Rest, through the sacred doorway of the west.*

Fig. 3: The Seal of Departing

The Seal of Protection

The purpose of this seal is to evoke/invoke the protective power of your Familiar whenever you have need of it. It is used in combination with the Seal of Calling. The Seal of Protection features the mystical hand of divinity appearing from a cloud. The cloud represents the manifestation of spiritual forces in the magical ether. The divine hand holds a pentagram, the symbol of the four elements brought into harmony by the intervention of spiritual forces. Three spirals appear at the command of the divine hand, for three is the mystical number of manifestation. The spirals represent the forces of transformation.

A series of words of power inscribed in the Witches' alphabet encircles the seal. Each word is separated by a star, symbolizing the astral forces at work. The spoken words of invocation for this seal are:

> My foe, *whatever to this place you send,*
> *The elements do wholly rend.*

Fig. 4: The Seal of Protection

The Seal of Dreaming

The purpose of this seal is to either meet your Familiar in the Dream World where it can directly speak and communicate to you, or to have it assist you in any Dream Work you may need to perform. It is used in combination with the Seal of Calling (and, if needed, the Seal of Protection). The Seal of Dreaming features the mystical eye, which is set at the meeting place of two trian-gles. The triangle on top points upward, indicating manifestation on the astral plane. The triangle below symbolizes manifestation on the material plane. To each of the tips of the triangle is at-tached a crescent moon, symbolizing the lunar influence upon the Dream World. In three of the crescents a spiral appears, which symbolize transformation.

A series of words of power inscribed in the Witches' alphabet encircles the seal. Each word is separated by a star, symbolizing the astral forces at work. The spoken words of invocation for this seal are:

> *All signs and omens do dreams reveal,*
> *The truth to the sleeper beneath this seal.*

Fig. 5: The Seal of Dreaming

The Seal of Carrying a Spell

The purpose of this seal is to have your Familiar convey the magical energy of a spell to your target. It is used in combination with the Seal of Calling. The Seal of Carrying a Spell features a sphere, above which appears a pair of wings. The sphere represents a thought-form or cohesive magical projection containing one's desired manifestation. The wings symbolize the astral substance that envelops energy and carries the process toward manifestation. Three spirals appear on the seal and symbolize the power of transformation.

A series of words of power inscribed in the Witches' alphabet encircles the seal. Each word is separated by a star, symbolizing the astral forces at work. The spoken words of invocation for this seal are:

> Carry my wishes on winged breast,
> And thereby desire is made manifest.

Fig. 6: The Seal of Carrying a Spell

The Seal of Protection Against Unwanted Familiars

The purpose of this seal is to ward off any unwanted Familiar that may be sent to you. This seal features the mystical hand of divinity appearing from a cloud. The cloud represents the manifestation of spiritual forces in the magical ether. Three spirals appear at the command of the divine hand, for three is the mystical number of manifestation. The spirals represent the forces of transformation. The hand appears in the gesture of stopping whatever approaches. An X appears encircled in the palm of the hand, symbolizing control over life and death. This speaks of caution against ignoring the warning that appears, for the hand is poised to seize and enclose.

A series of words of power inscribed in the Witches' alphabet encircles the seal. Each word is separated by a star, symbolizing the astral forces at work. The spoken words of invocation for this seal are:

> Strict charge I give and do hold fast,
> For beyond this point you shall not pass!

Fig. 7: The Seal of Protection Against Unwanted Familiars

The Seal of Severance

The purpose of this seal is to completely dissolve all magical, spiritual, emotional, physical, psychic, and mental connections between you and your Familiar. The Seal of Severance features the mystical hand of divinity appearing from a cloud. The cloud represents the manifestation of spiritual forces in the magical ether. Three spirals appear at the command of the divine hand, for three is the mystical number of manifestation. The spirals represent the forces of transformation. The hand holds a sickle, the tool of cutting down what has grown to fullness. This symbolizes the ending of existence in the material realm.

A series of words of power inscribed in the Witches' alphabet encircle the seal. Each word is separated by a star, symbolizing the astral forces at work. The spoken words of invocation for this seal are:

> All things in their time must pass away,
> And for you the sickle comes today.

Fig. 8: The Seal of Severance

The Seal of Binding

The purpose of this seal is to fix or attach your Familiar to a specific person, place, or thing, allowing it to remain for longer periods within the material plane. The Familiar is typically bound to a representative statue or figurine. Used in combination with the Seal of Calling, the Seal of Binding features a serpent twisting around two triangles, symbolizing the occult principle of manifestation. The triangle on top points upward, indicating manifestation on the astral plane. The triangle below symbolizes manifestation on the material plane. The serpent is a creature of the Underworld, the realm of procreation from which all things issue forth. It symbolizes an active and directed force at work between and within the planes. Flanking the primary design are three spirals representing magical forces pressing inward upon the occult principle of binding.

A series of words of power inscribed in the Witches' alphabet encircles the seal. Each word is separated by a star, symbolizing the astral forces at work. The spoken words of invocation for this seal are:

> *Wrapped and tied from within and without,*
> *From head to toe and all about.*

Fig. 9: The Seal of Binding

The Seal for Controlling an Errant Familiar

The purpose of this seal is bring a disruptive Familiar back into a harmonious relationship. It is used in combination with the Seal of Calling. The Seal for Controlling an Errant Familiar features the mystical hand of divinity appearing from a cloud. The cloud represents the manifestation of spiritual forces in the magical ether. The hand holds the three lightning bolts of the King of the Gods. In ancient myth the first bolt was a warning, the second could kill, and the third could destroy a world. Three spirals appear at the command of the divine hand, for three is the mystical number of manifestation. The spirals represent the forces of transformation.

A series of words of power inscribed in the Witches' alphabet encircles the seal. Each word is separated by a star, symbolizing the astral forces at work. The spoken words of invocation for this seal are:

> Heed the gods' warning of lightning and thunder,
> Lest for your defiance they tear you asunder.

Fig. 10: The Seal for Controlling an Errant Familiar

The Seal of the Vortex

The purpose of this seal is to undo any of the other seals, or any situation caused by the other seals. It can also serve as an emergency "shutdown" should things go badly astray. The Seal of the Vortex features a winged entity bearing an amulet with an X engraved in its center. Beneath this appears a sphere with a spiral collapsing inward. Rushing into the vortex are four triangles marked with the chevron symbol of regeneration. The symbols represent the four elements of earth, air, fire, and water. Surrounding all the imagery are three spirals of transformation.

A series of words of power are inscribed in the Witches' alphabet and encircle the seal. The spoken words of invocation for this seal are:

> *The elements all dissolve away,*
> *And leave you Nothing in which to stay.*
> *To the nothingness return, by moon and sun,*
> *Through Witches' magic be you now undone!*

The Vortex Seal is not one of the nine seals that you will charge using the cord. To charge this seal you must perform the following. Begin the process by placing a fire-resistant metal cup out beneath the full moon when the moon is in the sign of Aries, Leo, or Sagittarius. Pour some personal cologne or perfume into the cup, about a third full. You can also use Everclear, which is a high alcohol-content liquor.

Let the moonlight fall upon it for a few moments, and blow across the surface of the liquid. Following this, carefully light the liquid with a long match. Extend your right hand up to the moon, cupping your palm just below it. With your left hand,

Fig. 11: The Seal of the Vortex

point your index finger directly at the flame and recite these
words:

> *Sigil, form, and will's desire,*
> *Dissolve away in magic fire,*
> *All I name is drawn into you,*
> *To pass away from this world's view.*

Take the Vortex Seal and quickly pass it through the flames
three times, each time saying:

> *By the Lady—may moonlight join with sacred*
> *Fame, and undo by magic all that I name.*

When not in use, take the seal and wrap it in a piece of silk.

Using the Magical Seals

With the exception of the Genesis Seal and the Seal for Carrying a Spell, all of the other seals can be protected with a coating
of Modge-podge or some other hobby-craft coating material.
Clay seals can be kept in a box or jar to avoid incidents that can
produce accidental marks in the substance. When the full moon
occupies the signs of Cancer, Scorpio, or Pisces, you can recharge
the seals with moonlight using the technique provided for the
Genesis Seal. You can use the original moon water as well, and
anoint the seal if a coated material protects it. If the seal is
unprotected, you can boil the water and quickly pass the seal
through the steam three times.

For magical purposes some of the seals are used individually
and some are combined with others. In certain circumstances a
seal must be used to counter the actions of another seal. An example is the Seal of Binding, which attaches a Familiar to something. To permanently release it would require the Seal of
Departing in order to free it from having to return to an object,

place, or person. In such a case, the binding would be undone and the previous magical charge becomes negated.

In usage, the Seal of Binding can be placed upon a statue or figurine, which is the most common technique. The Familiar is verbally directed to take up residence within the image. Visualizing it as a sphere moving into the figure follows this, and then the words of invocation are spoken while you point at the image.

To use a seal, hold it in your left hand (the hand of receiving) and look directly at the seal. Observe and concentrate on its symbolism for few moments as described in this book, and then speak the words of invocation. The seals are generally to be used in combination with the techniques in chapter three that address working with your Familiar. Each seal serves a different purpose, and you will want to study the symbolism on the seals in order to decide how, when, and for what purpose you want to use them. The following brief overview will help direct you, but eventually you will discover many other uses for the seals on your own.

The Seal of Calling is used with all of the seals in order to consciously add the power of your Familiar to the work at hand. Together with the Seal of Protection, your Familiar can be directed to stand guard in accord with your needs. The protection seal can be placed in your house while you're away, on some personal property you wish to keep safe during your absence, or it can be carried in your purse or wallet for personal protection. To protect you while dreaming or during astral projection you can place the seal above your bed.

The Seal of Carrying a Spell requires placing the sigilized name of your Familiar in the inner sphere of the seal beneath the wings. This is drawn with the charged pencil. Beneath the name, and still inside the sphere, place a sigil of the essence of your spell's desire. For example, if you are sending healing energy to a friend or loved one, you can sigilize the word "heal." If you desire, you can also draw a small image of your Familiar in the sphere along with the name. Essentially the magical image and connection you're making with this seal is that your Familiar is being transported to the target along with the energy of the spell.

The Seal of Dreaming can be placed above your bed, or you can wear it in some fashion. A plastic-covered name badge from an office supply store can be used to protect the seal from being damaged while worn in your sleep. Insert the seal into the case and pin the name badge to your clothing or even to your pillow or blanket. It is an old belief among Witches that Familiar spirits make direct contact in the Dream World. Here they can answer questions or "report" to you things that you may wish to know about.

Using the Seal of Calling, you can send out your Familiar to observe a situation, track something down, locate stolen objects, or whatever you desire. In sending off your Familiar, instruct it to report its findings to you in a dream. Then you can use the Dream Seal before drifting off to sleep, and specifically state, "Tonight I will meet my Familiar and receive the information I requested. I will remember the dream and awake with full clarity and recollection." Look at the seal after the affirmation, speak your Familiar's name, and then go to sleep. Do not give the matter further thought, as this tends to ground the energy needed to accomplish the desired affect.

The Seal of Protection Against Unwanted Familiars can be duplicated in order to provide several wards for different areas. It is necessary to press the copies together with the original. The occult principle here is called "contagion magic." This means that any thing coming into contact with another thing creates a discharge of energy, and both things receive a portion of the energy of each other. Clip the seals together with a plastic clip (do not use metal) and leave them pressed together for about twenty minutes to an hour. To rid yourself of unwanted Familiars sent to you by other people, place the seals in every window of your home (facing outward) each night for seven nights in a row. Do this every time you sense an intrusion.

The Seal of Severance is used in combination with the Seal of Departing, which is used before severing. When using the severance seal you must dissolve the Genesis Seal afterward to complete the process. Use the severance seal following the dissolving of artificial Familiars and thought-form Familiars discussed in chapters three and four. Relationships with Familiars can create deep connections within one's psyche, and it is best to sever ties when you no longer wish to work with a specific Familiar.

The Seal of Departing can be used to return your Familiar to the Otherworld when not in use. It can also be used to release the spirit of a pet who has died. This seal does not sever the relationship, nor does it interfere with the connection between human and Familiar. It functions more like a doorway and a formal "farewell until we meet again." Before dissolving the Genesis Seal, use the Seal of Departing to release the Familiar, followed by the Seal of Severance, and then burn the Genesis Seal, or bury it in the soil. Do not burn or bury the Genesis Seal while the Familiar is still linked to it.

The Seal of the Vortex is an emergency device designed to quickly close down a magical work that has gone astray, and to negate the actions of any of the other seals. To begin the process set the seal you wish to deactivate in front of you. Fix your gaze on the Seal of the Vortex and study its symbolism. Next, look at the other seal and visualize a sphere of energy around it. Then speak the words of invocation for the vortex seal, and visualize the sphere being pulled into the vortex seal. Visualize the spiral, pulling it down into the center where it disappears. Once you use the Seal of the Vortex on another seal the energy of that seal will be gone and it will no longer function reliably.

You can also use the vortex seal to rid yourself of unwanted entities that intrude into your home. When you sense a presence, visualize a sphere of light encasing it. Then look at the Vortex Seal, speak the words of invocation, and visualize the sphere being drawn into it.

Ethics

A Witch lives by a personal code of ethics rooted in self-responsibility, magical principles, and the ways of Nature. The average Witch lives by the old philosophy of "live and let live." He or she accepts that everyone has the right to believe in whatever works for them, and the Witch strives to live in peaceful coexistence within his or her community.

It is neither the goal nor the desire of the average Witch to cause harm to the innocent. Equally there is no inclination to bring disharmony to the lives of others, nor does the desire exist to wish ill will upon others. However, the Witch is not by nature one who "turns the other cheek" when attacked or abused. For the Witch it is all about living life in balance. This includes restoring balance in the life of the Witch when others have disrupted it.

Before closing this chapter it seems appropriate to say a few words about the ethics of using seals and Familiars. There are several issues to consider here. The first is whether it is right to call upon Familiar spirits. The argument can be made that calling upon a Familiar to aid you is really no different ethically than calling upon the elementals to help you cast your circle, or to empower your spells.

The second issue concerns using Familiars in connection with other people. Many people feel that a person should not even perform a healing without the knowledge and permission of the other person. The counterargument can be made that if a person sees his or her friend about to be harmed by something coming up from behind, and does nothing to interfere with it, then nonaction results in harm. Here one must discern what type of friend one wishes to be.

Some people feel that it is wrong to harm even someone who is trying to harm you. The core issue here is the belief that a person should never impose his or her will upon another. However, involving yourself in the affairs of another is, from an occult perspective, a matter of intent. Intent is the energy that binds karma to a soul. For example, killing an enemy in battle invokes a different karmic debt than killing a store clerk during a holdup. The energy and the intent of the killer is quite different, and the ripple of energy would certainly draw a different "karmic imprint" or response in return.

With a little thought it is evident that as a society we impose our will on people in very significant ways. For example, people who commit crimes such as robbery, rape, or murder do so out of personal will. It is what they want to do, choose to do, or feel compelled to do. We put people like this in prison and deny them their personal will to harm us further. In prison they live in a dangerous environment in which they can be injured or killed at any time. Therefore, we have, in effect, harmed them by imprisoning them in this environment. Sometimes it is necessary and beneficial to impose one's will upon another, although it is never desirable nor pleasant.

All debates aside, the reality is that the day will come when you will either need to protect yourself or someone you care about from magical or psychic attack. The attack may originate from another practitioner, or it may come from the Otherworld. My personal feelings are that defending yourself with your magical abilities is a reasonable alternative to victimization and personal harm. However, in the end only you can decide whether you will live as a victim or as a participant in the affairs of your own life.

Whether to launch a defensive counterattack is a matter that deserves a great deal of consideration. While you can instead deplete your energy by continuously erecting protections and magically charging them, this will eventually create more problems for you (including health issues due to exhaustion and emotional stress). This is because the protections you create will continue to draw upon your own energy in order to maintain their effectiveness. When an attacker is persistent you may indeed find it necessary to counterattack in self-defense.

In the next chapter we will explore the relationship with a Familiar Spirit. Here we will find the Familiar as a companion and an ally in our magical world. Let us turn now and discover how we can create this alliance between human and Familiar spirit.

3

RELATIONSHIP
WITH THE
FAMILIAR

Witches have always respected life in any and all forms. It is very natural for a Witch to talk to his or her pet as one might speak to a visiting friend. Witches know that all life forms are equal, as is everything in Nature. We are all one, inseparably linked in the cycles of life and death. It is often difficult for non-Witches to understand this pagan mentality. If you add this to a superstitious era of humankind you can begin to see what happened during the time of the Inquisition.

Many people in the Witchcraft/Wiccan community today obtain physical pets and enter into a psychic relationship with them. This is excellent, and has many rewarding aspects, but differs from the original concept of the Familiar. It is difficult to define a Familiar today, because they are various things to various people. In this book I will focus more on the time-honored concept of the Familiar as preserved in authentic Witchlore as opposed to the Familiar as depicted by the Church during the Middle Ages and Renaissance period.

Once you have performed the exercise in chapter two you will know the form that your Familiar has chosen as its vehicle. It is then time to begin the bonding process. The first step is to research the animal whose image appeared to you (or with whom you have had a long-term attraction/fascination). There is a reason why the Familiar chose the particular form in which it appeared to you. There is something in the nature of the animal that is a key to power for you, or whose symbolic nature will have a transformative influence in your life. Search it out and you will find it.

The second step is to learn to summon the Familiar. Part of this involves what I call "embracing" the Familiar, which is covered later in this chapter. At some point you may choose to obtain a physical representation of the Familiar, so that your bonding with the Spirit is affirmed in the Physical Plane. This is the origin of the Witch and her or his pet Familiar. If it is not practical or possible for you to obtain a living creature, then you can use a photo, painting, or statue/figurine. This will serve as a focal point for working with the Familiar within the material world.

When working with the physical Familiar you will actually be using the astral form of the animal, and only to a lesser extent the physical form. Once you have established rapport you will be able to merge with your Familiar. In a merged state you can then communicate with and direct the spirit consciousness of the animal. Bear in mind that this is a mutually advantageous relationship and not one of servant and master.

From an occult perspective, various elements of personal consciousness are exchanged during the merging experience. Through this technique both parties temporarily receive the imprint of a different nature. The human is aligned with the primal consciousness, and the ancient nature is awakened within the mind. This is both vitalizing and empowering for the human. Through merging, the animal is aligned with human reasoning and creativity. This expands the consciousness of the animal and stimulates the mind of the animal to see and reason in different ways.

Merging with the Familiar

To begin the process of merging with your physical Familiar you will need to use something that the animal enjoys in order to make the animal receptive. Petting a cat or dog in a quiet setting is one example. For the purposes of this chapter I'm going to use the cat as the model for working with animals. Most techniques will apply to other creatures, and if you know your animal well enough you can adapt and modify the exercises accordingly.

Not all animals will allow direct eye contact, and with dogs it can be taken as a sign of aggression. However, the eyes are the best access points through which to merge consciousness. An alternative is using the breath to make access through the nose. A soft and slow exhale toward the face of the animal will carry your energy and directed thoughts.

Animals communicate on a "formed thought" level. They think in visual images rather than in language, as we understand it. Therefore, mental images can be sent to them by the mind. By forming clear mental images of what you wish to communicate to your Familiar, you can instruct it as to what you desire the Familiar to perform. Keep the images simple. Using the cat as an example, try picturing in your mind the image of your cat walking over to you and jumping into your lap. Look at the cat, and run the scene in your mind several times. Try this at various times of the day, each day, until it becomes apparent that the cat is responding to your mental images.

Because animals are sensitive to energy, they are also sensitive to tones. Each animal has an affinity for certain sounds. Try using different tones, humming them, and observe the animal's reaction. You want to find a tone that is soothing and does not disturb the animal. Use this tone while petting the animal in order to aid with alignment. Petting an animal exchanges energy between the animal and the human. In effect, it communicates directly with the aura where it causes changes to occur by enhancing the energy field.

Petting is also an effective technique for charging the animal's fur with a magical intent. You can even charge someone else's pet using this technique and, for example, imprint healing energy. As the person pets the animal, the healing energy will be absorbed from the fur. Other intentions can be set in place as well. The basic concept involves forming a thought into a desire, and the desire into an energy form. The energy form is then directed into a target where it awaits release. For further information see the section in this chapter and in chapter four for creating thought-forms.

Once you feel that mental communication between you and the Familiar is established to some degree, then you can begin the merging process. This requires physical contact with the Familiar. While holding or petting the Familiar, mentally see the animal separate into a spirit/astral double. Then mentally see this form move into your body and blend into your being. Picture yourself as taking on its form as though you were shapeshifting. Then create an imaginary journey in which you travel as the animal and perform the magical acts required to accomplish the goal you desire. Once completed, mentally see the spirit/astral double of the animal leave you and return to the physical Familiar. When the animal sleeps, its astral form will do as you imagined in your journey.

A basic example of a magical journey may help illustrate the principle of working with Familiars in their spirit/astral form. If you wish someone with whom you have lost contact to contact you, you can send your Familiar to them through directed imagery. In the case of the cat, see the cat slip into their home through the door or window. It doesn't matter that you may not know where they live. Next, have the cat pick up their phone in its mouth and carry it to them. The cat can "meow" your name to them or even speak clearly. You can do the same thing with a bird or dog, etc. Repeat the process previously described several times over the course of a few days. Instead of a phone you can substitute a pen and paper for a letter. With a little imagination you might even be able to evoke an e-mail!

Because of the special relationship that exists between you and your Familiar, you will need to magically charge its food in order to maintain a strong alignment with the Familiar. This is very simple and easy to do. Simply put some food in a bowl and then form an energy sphere, passing it into the food and leaving it in place. Instructions for creating an energy sphere appear in chapter four. When the animal consumes the food, the Familiar will absorb some of your energy. This will strengthen the bond between the two of you, and ensure loyalty.

Other techniques for working with physical Familiars can be drawn from the next section dealing with nonphysical Familiars. The spirit or astral double of the physical Familiar can be incorporated into the techniques and concepts covered in the following material.

Working with the
Nonphysical Familiar

The nonphysical Familiar is easier to work with, as you will not
have to deal with the mundane aspects and requirements of a
physical animal. Whether the Familiar is a spirit, astral entity, or
an artificial Familiar you will need a device to house it in while
working with it within the material dimension. This is covered
in the following sections of this chapter.

The instructions provided in the remaining material in this
chapter deal with the Familiar that you contacted through the
exercise given in chapter two. This entity may be an astral being
or a spirit from the Otherworld. For the purposes of the exercises
provided here, the nature of the Familiar will not be a factor.

Summoning the Familiar

This technique is a more advanced use of the Seal of Calling. In
preparation for summoning your Familiar use the Seal of Calling
from chapter two. When you desire to call your Familiar, follow
the instructions for using the seal, and then pick up your power
stone (left hand) and visualize it glowing white. Visualize the
opening to the cave you saw in the guided meditation journey.
This cave leads to the Inner World where the Familiar abides.
Extend your hand straight out before you, palm facing up. Mentally, or verbally, speak the name of your Familiar, saying in a re-
spectful tone: "Come _____."

Then visualize the image of your Familiar, as was revealed to
you in the Inner World journey. See the Familiar appear before
you in your mind's eye. Next visualize it glowing white, and draw
it totally into your body, absorbing it so that the two of you are
now one, glowing together in white light.

To direct the Familiar at this point, simply condense it into a
sphere of light, focused in your personal power center just below

the navel, and mentally move it out of your body (see techniques in chapter four). You can pass the energy sphere into a physical form such as a statue, a charm or talisman, or whatever you feel is appropriate to the work at hand. You may even wish to have the Familiar remain within you for personal empowerment. Make sure to release the Familiar when the work is completed. Under no circumstances should you keep the Familiar within yourself as a permanent or even long-term measure.

Embracing the Familiar

After summoning the Familiar into your own being you must "embrace" it. This does not have to be performed every time you summon it, but must be done at least once a week. If you do not, then you may lose connection with your Familiar. This phase is essential in order to possess a Familiar spirit.

To begin, visualize the image of the Familiar as though it is a costume you are wearing. Begin to sense what it might feel like to be that animal or creature. Now you must begin to act out the nature of the animal. Move as you might imagine the animal moves, and be like it as much as possible. In essence you want to become the animal on every level that you can. Through this technique it will become "Familiar" to you and you will truly be one together. This is, in part, what it means to possess a Familiar Spirit.

License to Depart

When you have completed working with your Familiar then it is time to return it to the Otherworld. To do this, use the Seal of Departing (chapter two) and then visualize the cave opening that originally led you to the Familiar. Mentally send the Familiar into the cave, instructing it to return home until it is needed again. You may find it useful to devise a series of hand gestures or positions to represent the opening and the closing of the portals.

These hand gestures/positions will then be used with each of the appropriate visualizations for "coming" and "returning."

If desired you can recite the License to Depart in addition to the visualizations. Simply speak these words:

> (Name), *I thank you for your aid,*
> *And as you depart now unto your realm,*
> *May there always be peace between us.*
> *I bid thee now farewell.*

Naming the Familiar

If the Familiar did not reveal its name during the "journey" phase then it will most likely respond to any name that you choose. If you feel uncomfortable with simply naming the Familiar, then you can try the following:

Take a group of small stones and print a letter of the alphabet upon each stone. You can also use Scrabble squares for this purpose. Turn the square letter-side down, so that only the blank sides are visible. Next, mix the stones completely to ensure a random order. Using the numerical value chart below, take your own name (first and last) and reduce it numerically. An example follows using the imaginary name of Paul Saxon:

A, J, S   =   1
B, K, T   =   2
C, L, U   =   3
D, M, V   =   4
E, N, W   =   5
F, O, X   =   6
G, P, Y   =   7
H, Q, Z   =   8
I, R   =   9

P   a   u   l   S   a   x   o   n
7   1   3   3   1   1   6   6   5

Add the numbers of the first name and reduce to the lowest numerical value:

P   a   u   l
7 + 1 + 3 + 3 = 14
14 = 1 + 4 = 5

Do the same with the last name:

S   a   x   o   n
1 + 1 + 6 + 6 + 5 = 19
19 = 1 + 9 = 10
1 + 0 = 1

Now take the value of the first and last name, and add them together (reducing to the lowest numerical value):

1 (Saxon) + 5 (Paul) = 6

In the case of Paul Saxon, he would then choose six of the lettered stones at random and place them side by side from left to right. Looking at the letters, he would take note of any name suggested by the order of letters. If the stones do not seem to reveal a name, then the six stones are arranged in different patterns to form a name of some type. Ultimately this would continue until a name is discernable from the letters that appear. This may require some imagination as well as practicing alternative pronunciations.

Working with the Familiar

There are many different ways in which a Familiar may be used. In this section we will examine a few techniques, but feel free to experiment with your own methods. Whenever distance is an issue, you can use the Seal of Carrying a Spell (chapter two) to transport your Familiar where it needs to go. This is particularly useful if your Familiar animal has no wings or is not noted for speed or endurance in travel.

For Healing

Visualize either the projected Familiar sphere or the projected image resting upon the area that requires healing. Next, mentally direct the Familiar down into the area using either mental images or verbal instruction in the work to be done. After a few moments visualize the area glowing with healing energy. The color of the glow can be visualized in a symbolic color, appropriate to the desired effect. Generally speaking, yellow is stimulating, green soothing, blue cleansing, and red vitalizing.

Allow the Familiar to work for at least fifteen minutes. You can add any of your own healing techniques at this point, and work along with the Familiar. When you are ready, recall the Familiar by visualizing its withdrawal or summoning with the Seal of Calling. Do not embrace the Familiar following its withdrawal. Instead, send it some energy from your power stone (visualizing a glowing sphere, moving from the stone to the Familiar). Then give "license to depart," returning the Familiar to its own realm. You will probably need to call upon the Familiar several times for the healing work, depending on the seriousness of the illness of injury.

For Magic

There are many magical uses of the Familiar. A Familiar can carry the energy of a spell to someone or some place if you desire. It can obtain information for you on the inner planes (physical or astral), or serve as a guardian. I will give you a basic outline for working magic with your Familiar, and later you can expand or modify this in order to formulate your own techniques.

First you must summon the Familiar, and mentally (or verbally) instruct it according to your desire. Always remember that this entity is a separate being having its own existence. It assists you in accord with the bond that you have created. Once summoned, move the Familiar to your cupped palms. Visualize a sphere-of-energy formed in your palms, and then speak your instructions into the sphere.

Once instructed, it is best to visualize the Familiar with wings. Make a copy of the Astral Gateway image (below) and prop it up on the west side of your altar. Color the ring around the portal sphere purple, for this is the magical color of the moon. The Astral Gateway (below) can be used as a doorway for the Familiar to leave this dimension and access the inner planes. This will allow

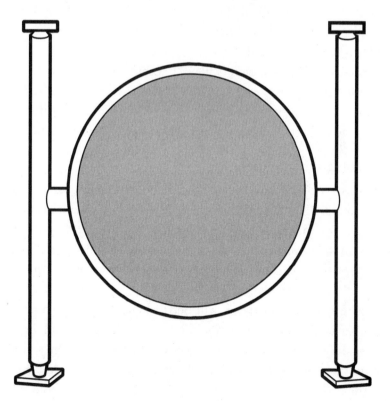

Fig. 12: The Astral Gateway

it to fly upon the planes and easily perform its task. You may wish to use the Seal of Carrying a Spell along with this technique.

The Familiar can be visualized as a winged sphere or as a creature with wings. You will soon know if the Familiar objects to either form, as your visualization will quickly break down. To send the Familiar off, mentally see it enter the Astral Gateway, and then visualize it flying away in the direction of the target. You will need to visualize its journey, as though you were traveling with it, and see it reach its target goal. Mentally direct it to establish the desired purpose. After working with your Familiar for several months, this phase will no longer be necessary. This is because the Familiar will quickly learn on its own from your example.

You will find it effective to mentally give the Familiar a sigil to carry with it that is symbolic of the magical affect, or desired end result. The Familiar can then place the sigil upon the person (or place) to be influenced.

Generally, "information" will be "transmitted" to you by the Familiar through dreams or "psychic impressions." Use the Seal of Dreaming for this purpose (chapter two). Only through experience will you learn the full powers and limitations of your Familiar.

Housing the Familiar

This is a technique for keeping the Familiar in the physical plane for a longer period of time than required for any given task. The Familiar can then be used for lengthy healing work without having to summon it again and again. It can also serve as a "guardian" during astral projection, deep meditation, dream work, and so on.

The first thing that you will need is another power stone of the same type used to summon the Familiar. Next you will need to make or obtain an image statue of your Familiar. The statue must be hollowed out, with a hole at the base for later drainage. If the object is solid, you can carefully drill a hole. This hole will be sealed until the Familiar is released. A ceramic animal bank (the so-called "piggy bank") can easily be used for this purpose, after sealing off the money slot. A cork or some type of plug can be used to seal the hole, and melted wax should be poured over it to further secure the seal.

Place the extra power stone inside the image, and fill the image with the four elemental condensers about two-thirds full. Examples of condensers can be found in this chapter in the section dealing with "artificial Familiars." Use equal measured parts of each condenser. Next you will need to place three drops of your blood into the image. This will provide the Familiar with your own vital energy, which will help it to maintain its presence in the physical plane.

Extra power may be added by placing fresh semen or vaginal secretions within the image. If these sexually produced fluids are used, you must remember that any mental images you formed during sexual stimulation have left their energy-print in the magnetic fluid. These energies will influence the Familiar to varying degrees, and can operate like subconscious thoughts for the Familiar. Therefore try and stay purely focused on the intent of the magical goal.

Now the image/statue can be prepared to receive the Familiar spirit. Make sure that the image/statue is tightly sealed to avoid any leakage. Summon the Familiar, then transfer it through visualization into the image/statue. Whenever you need the Familiar, simply summon it and mentally draw it out through visualization, then direct it off. Always order it to return to the image each night at a specific and stated time. Remember to give it all the necessary instruction in accord with your magical desire. Always include the purpose, who or what the target is, the amount of time it will be away, what the goal is, and the instruction to return to the image that you created.

To release the Familiar back to its realm once the relationship is severed, use the method of pouring out liquids given in the closing of the next section on the artificial Familiar.

The Artificial Familiar

The method of creating an artificial Familiar is the same as "housing" the Familiar given previously, with only a few differences. The advantage of using this technique is simply that it is less involved than obtaining a spirit or astral Familiar entity.

Once you have the statue that you have chosen to represent the nature of your Familiar, then proceed as follows: Stand before the object (having already filled it with the prescribed liquids, with the seal in place) and begin to raise an energy sphere between your palms. Draw this energy from your base chakra located in the genital region. Bring the energy up to your personal power center (just below the navel), and project it out into your palms. Visualize an image of your Familiar appearing within the sphere.

Once formed, mentally transfer the sphere into the statue. Then pick it up and exhale upon it three times. As you do this, state that you are giving it the breath of life. Visualize a blue light passing into the statue, and mentally see the object glowing. The Familiar is now ready to be instructed.

An elemental Familiar should only be allowed to remain for a period of seven days. If it is allowed to remain longer it may begin to take on a will of its own and begin drawing energy from you in order to sustain itself. Therefore you should verbally instruct the Familiar, stating that it will cease to exist on the seventh day.

After four days have passed (each time thereafter that the Familiar is sent off) you must then perform the following action: Each day, for the next three days, you will pour out a small portion of the fluid directly upon the earth. Make sure that you still have some liquid to pour out on the last day, which is the seventh day. You have a bond with the Familiar on every level, and pouring out the essence will drain some of your own energy as well. Therefore, do not pour out all of the liquid at once—you must take the full three days.

Upon completion use the Seal of Departing and the Seal of Severance. See chapter five for further information and instruction.

The Elemental Condensers

These fluids are charged with the various elemental influences and are used to add extra potency to spells and other magical workings. First you will need the following substances:

Fire: Chili pepper juice, or "hot sauce" made from peppers. A red color is best, if possible.

Air: A mild brew of mint tea.

Earth: Mineral oil.

Water: Cucumber juice or watermelon juice (any melon will do).

Once you have these substances then you will begin to prepare them as follows.

Take four small bottles and pour a different fluid into each one. Label or make the bottles according to the corresponding element. Next absorb and project the appropriate element into the bottle (see Absorption and Projection of Elements). Once this is completed then you will connect these fluids to their physical counterparts as follows.

Fire Condenser: pass the bottle through a flame for a couple of minutes, concentrating upon the element.

Air Condenser: suspend the bottle from a tree (or any high place) so that it hangs in the air for a time. Concentrate upon the element.

Earth Condenser: bury the bottle in soil for a time, concentrating upon the element. Afterward you will retrieve
the bottle.

Water Condenser: place the bottle in a natural body of
water (lake, ocean, stream), concentrating upon the element. Afterward you will retrieve the bottle.

Because of the magnetic properties (or quality) of liquids,
these bottled fluids will absorb and contain the magical essences
of the elements. It is the etheric materials that become
condensed.

Absorption and Projection of Elements

This exercise (and technique) is very important to the art of
magical influence. It is through this absorption (condensation)
and projection of the elements that certain metaphysical forces
are drawn toward manifestation.

Exercises/Techniques

1. *Absorbing Fire:* Sit comfortably and imagine yourself in
   the center of a sphere of fire (nothing exists but you and
   the sphere). Inhale, imagining that this fire is drawn
   into your body. Draw it into your entire being. Imagine
   that you are hollow and are being filled with fire. Imagine the heat, the energy, the force. Count with a beaded
   string or necklace as you draw each breath, keeping
   track of how many times you inhale until you are filled
   with fire.

   While you are inhaling an element imagine the desired characteristic that corresponds to it. Mentally fix
   it and emotionally fix it. Once you have completed this
   stage, then visualize yourself (inside and out) glowing
   red. Now you are ready to project the element. Exhale
   upon the object you wish to charge, visualizing the

color pouring out and the object glowing with it. Imagine the heat pouring out also. With each act of exhaling, count again with the beaded string or necklace. You must exhale exactly as many times as you have inhaled.

2. *Absorbing Air:* This is performed in the same manner as was fire, except for the following: Imagine the sensation of growing lighter. Do not imagine any temperature changes. The color for visualization in this element is blue.

3. *Absorbing Water:* Do the same for this method as was done for the others, with the following exceptions: Imagine the sensation of coldness filling you. Become heavy but fluid, feel the weight of movement (not stability as with earth). The color to associate with water is green.

4. *Absorbing Earth:* This is performed in the same manner as the other elements with the following exceptions: Imagine the sensation of weight, feel the loose soil pouring in (like the sand in an hourglass). Do not imagine clay earth, as this substance has water in it. Do not imagine a temperature change. The color for earth is yellow.

Now that we have explored some of the techniques for creating a relationship with a Familiar, it is time to examine the different ways Familiars can work with us. In the following chapter you will not only encounter the different roles a Familiar can play, you will also be introduced to some expanded and more detailed methods related to the concepts you learned in this present chapter.

4

THE GUARDIAN
FAMILIAR

The path of Witchcraft leads one into the realm of magic. Working magic attracts spirits from the Otherworld. Some of these spirits can attach themselves to your home and ritual area, and may chose not to leave. Others may return at a time of their own choosing. Generally speaking this is not a desirable situation and you will want to be alert to any such comings and goings. On occasion you may also find that another Witch is sending something your way that you do not want around you. Every religion has those who adhere to the ethics and spirituality of their path and those who do not.

Among the services provided by the Familiar on behalf of the Witch, the Familiar acts as a "sound of warning" and as a guardian. The sharp physical sense of hearing credited to many animals is but a reflection of their attunement to other realms. The Familiar aids the Witch by using its heightened senses to extend the awareness of the Witch. Anyone with a cat as a pet has frequently observed it seemingly chasing invisible things around the room and up the walls. From an occult perspective the cat is encountering entities from the spirit world or astral realm.

Some Witches work with their pets as Familiars, and in this sense such animals can be regarded as household guardians. To help empower the physical guardian you can use a permanent marker pen and draw the amulet design for the Familiar on the inside of the pet's collar. A small crystal should then be suspended on the collar to hold a magical charge. Techniques for charging and empowering can be found in part two of this chapter.

Many Witches work with astral or spirit Familiars as guardians and some use what is called the artificial Familiar. Such entities require a physical form in order to remain within the material dimension. This can be likened to having a fish in your home, which requires an environment to house it in. In the case of a fish this would be a bowl of water or a filled aquarium. For the Familiar you can use a statue or figurine. If you wish to use a painting or drawing, consult the section in this chapter titled Dream Guardian.

Part One:
Home Guardian

Protecting the home is very important because this is your place of sanctuary from the outside world. Your home should offer you a feeling of comfort, safety, and rejuvenation. Therefore you will want to take steps toward keeping outside influences from penetrating your personal space. For further information outside the scope of this book, I refer the reader to my book *The Witches' Craft* (Llewellyn, 2002), which contains additional detailed instructions for protecting the home against magical attacks.

From a magical perspective there are two primary portals into a home. These entryways are the doors and the windows. The secondary entryways are the chimney opening and the plumbing pipes/fixtures within the house. These areas should be magically sealed and protected. Magical seals can be created physically on parchment and adhered to metal, clay, wood, or other substances. A good basic protection is the pentagram. Seals can also be created by visual imagery, tracing them either in the air (over the object) or directly on the object with a fingertip or athame. The advantage of drawing or etching one physically is that it requires less frequent recharging. Alone, the visual image will dissipate quicker since it lacks the form that allows longer cohesion within the material dimension.

The Pentagram spell works well for basic protections. You can use a physical pentagram or trace out an astral energy one. Trace a five-pointed star over the portal you wish to protect, visualize it as a blue-burning flame, and say these words:

> By spirit over matter,
> I bind here the forces
> Of earth, air, fire, and water.
> By spirit holding balance
> Over the four elements—
> Strict charge and watch I give,
> That through this opening
> No evil thing may approach
> Nor enter in.

Trace the star three times, and then trace a circle around the star three times as well. Repeating the incantation three times will help add extra power to the magical sealing.

In addition to magical seals and amulets, it is wise to place an image of one of your Familiars at each of the entryways into your home. Near the doors to your home (or just above them) place a representation of one of your Familiars that you deem most appropriate. You should also set a small figurine on each window ledge. As an alternative, a stained glass decoration can be suspended in the window. You can even hang a symbolic mobile near the window. In addition, place a representation of one of your Familiars in the kitchen and bathroom areas to protect the secondary levels of access.

These representations must be magically charged in order to empower them. Then each one must be recharged on the night of each full moon (before sunrise the following morning). The easiest way to do this is to charge an oil for protection beneath the full moon, and then anoint the images following the close of your ceremony. Use the same words of invocation as you did when visualizing the blue flame. See part two of this chapter for further information on magical charges.

Personal Protector

If you wish to have your Familiar travel with you when you are away from home, there are several techniques that will serve you. You can charge an amulet to wear or carry in your purse or pocket. This amulet should have the image of the Familiar on it. You can also simply charge a key ring, your watch, or some other metal object and visualize the Familiar's image in an energy form passing into the project. When needed in specific situations you can then call upon your Familiar.

I personally knew a Witch who worked extensively with a wolf figure as her Familiar. One late night while going to her car alone in an almost vacant parking lot, two men started to move in her direction. Concerned for her safety she continued to walk, evoked the wolf, and strongly visualized it in her company. As the men drew nearer she heard one say, "She's got a dog!" and they quickly moved off in the opposite direction.

From one occult perspective what the men saw was an astral image, the thought-form projected by the Witch. Another possibility is that the Familiar itself, as a conscious being, materialized to protect her. In effect, it doesn't really matter what the entity or phenomena was, it is important only that the Witch continued to her car unmolested.

Personal property items can also be protected from theft and damage by placing them under the protection of a Familiar. This includes anything left outside such as a car or a bicycle. This can be accomplished by placing the charged seal of the Familiar on the object. In the event that the object disappears, you can invoke your Familiar in order to track its location down. This requires performing the embracing rite and then waiting for visual images to appear while you meditate or dream. Most of the time Familiars will communicate to you in the Dream State. See chapter two for details about using the Seal of Dreaming.

A basic technique exists for establishing protective energy in the aura, and this can be used for personal empowerment or to shield yourself against attack from both physical and nonphysical opponents. The technique is called the Pentagram Posture.

To perform this work of magic, stand in the position shown in the illustration (p. 80). Connect with the indwelling divine spark within you, visualizing a brilliant white glowing sphere in your heart area. Then say:

> Though I am born of this world,
> My race is of the stars.

Now, visualize a glowing sphere of white light encompassing your head, and say:

> I call upon pure Spirit.
> As above, so below,
> as within, so without.

Fig. 13: The Elemental Pentagram Posture

Then, visualize a glowing sphere of green light encompassing your left hand, and say:

> *By the power of Spirit over the elements,*
> *I summon the pure essence of water.*

Next, visualize a glowing sphere of red light encompassing your left foot, and say:

> *By the power of Spirit over the elements,*
> *I summon the pure essence of fire.*

Now, visualize a glowing sphere of yellow light encompassing your right foot, and say:

> By the power of Spirit over the elements,
> I summon the pure essence of earth.

Then, visualize a glowing sphere of blue light encompassing your right hand, and say:

> By the power of Spirit over the elements,
> I summon the pure essence of air.

Finally, visualize yourself enclosed in a large sphere of glowing light, alternating with the colors you used for spirit, water, fire, earth, and air. Then visualize the sphere glowing white, and say:

> By the power of Spirit
> Joined with elements in balance,
> Here strict charge is given,
> That in my presence
> No evil thing may approach
> Nor enter in.

If you desire, you can add words to describe a certain situation or concern that you need to deal with. Then claim power over it by the intervention of spirit in harmony with the four elements. This is a powerful concept, and one that is reflected in the four Witches' tools that symbolize the elemental forces: the pentacle (earth), wand (air), athame (fire), and chalice (water). The assignment of elemental natures to the four tools differs according to cultural tradition or focus. Therefore, not every Witchcraft tradition uses the associations given here.

Dream Guardian

When a person is asleep and dreaming, he or she is the most receptive to magical influences and any mental energies that might be projected by others. Therefore it is wise to establish protections in the bedroom area. The Familiar can serve as a guardian in this manner. For such a purpose an image is required to "house" the Familiar in the bedroom as you sleep. You can also use a painting or drawing in a glass picture frame instead. The glass is required to hold the charge. The technique is described later in this section.

The image should be placed so that it faces you while you are asleep. Then you can activate it before going to bed (see Magical Charges in this chapter). To activate the image, simply anoint the image with protective oil and pass an "informed" thought-form into it. This will provide the instructions required for the Familiar to be of service while you sleep under its protection.

If you use a painting or a picture as a desired guardian figure, instead of a statue or figurine, then place it in a glass-covered frame to protect it. Do this on the day of the new moon. Then when the moon is full, coat the entire surface of the glass with one or more of the four elemental condensers:

Earth: salt dissolved in water.

Air: mint tea.

Fire: juice from a pepper.

Water: melon juice.

To employ a condenser simply select the elemental substance that best suits the nature of the desired goal. For example a shield can be assigned to the elemental nature of earth. A barrier can be assigned to the element of fire. Once you have decided upon which element or combination of elements you will employ, then put the elemental substances into a bottle.

Place the bottle in front of you and breathe in each one of the elements that you are going to be working with. To do this, mentally visualize the element in an active state. For earth this might be an earthquake, for air a strong wind, for fire a raging furnace, and for water a crashing wave or a powerful waterfall. After imagining each element individually, mentally transform each one into a color: yellow for earth, blue for air, red for fire, and green for water. Next, exhale each element separately into the bottle, visualizing your breath to be that color. As your breath passes into the bottle, visualize the contents glowing with the elemental color you exhaled.

When the elemental charge is completed pour some of the condenser or condensers into a glass (about half full) and let the glass sit for an hour. Then dip the tip of your finger in the glass of water and slide your finger across the surface of the glass. You will do this diagonally from edge to edge, making a large X figure across the glass pane. Following this, dab the same fingertip on the inside corner of the glass where it meets the picture frame. This will be the four ends of the X you first made. Performing this task will collect a combined portion of all the elemental condensers into four individual spots.

Next, take a damp (not dripping) cotton cloth and wipe the surface of the glass, leaving the four corners undisturbed. You do not want to remove the elemental condensers from the corners where you placed them by dabbing your fingertip. Next, dry the glass panel thoroughly while again avoiding the four corners. Now trace a pentagram over the glass with your athame or index finger, beginning at the top center and working down to the lower right point and continuing clockwise. As you trace the pentagram recite these words:

> By spirit light as a magic feather,
> I bring the four elements together.

> *Earth to shield from all attack,*
> *Air to the sender carries back.*
> *Water to cleanse the depth and height,*
> *Fire to empower it great with might.*

Now trace a circle around the pentagram star, saying as you do so:

> *Strict charge and watch I give, as I begin.*
> *No evil thing may approach nor enter in!*

Complete the spell by looking at the Familiar image and reciting:

> *Familiar spirit in the glass,*
> *With this star I bind you fast.*
> *The elements now do make the charm,*
> *Protect me all this night from harm.*

Place the image so that it can easily be seen should your bed be approached by anything during the night.

The Plant Familiar

Witches believe that everything has a consciousness, something imbued or apportioned by its creators. In some ancient cultures this consciousness was known as the *numen*. A numen provides the force that allows spirit to adhere to matter. The numen is what gives things a certain *feel*, which attracts or repels us. From an occult perspective the numen is the mystical and magical energy dwelling within. It is the occult property of any given thing. An occult property is the astral counterpart to the material nature. In other words it is the metaphysical versus the physical, the supernatural versus the natural.

For countless centuries Witches have drawn upon the numen power of herbs and other plants. The pharmaceutical properties of herbs are the counterparts to the metaphysical energy of any given herb. Long ago Witches ascribed a variety of attributes and associations to the herbs used in Witchcraft. These include planetary associations, seasonal connections, ruling deities, companion spirits, and magical powers.

Any plant can be used as a Familiar, and plants grown from seed make the most potent Familiar. The following technique is designed to transplant a plant that you wish to "raise," or grow a plant as a Familiar. Simply prepare the soil for planting in a secluded area, which is appropriate for the physical needs of the plant. Set a circle of small stones around the chosen plant in order to bind the numen in place. Dig a hole about six inches deep and place a power stone or crystal of your choosing in the

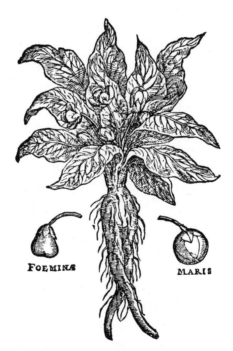

FOEMINA   MARIS

Fig. 14: The mandrake, because it resembled the human form, was used in magic and as a plant familiar (here depicted in a sixteenth-century woodcut © Dover, 1960).

hole to charge the plant with extra energy. Set the plant in the hole, cover with soil, and leave the plant undisturbed for twenty-four hours.

You may wish to create several different plants to serve as Familiars, or you may wish to grow several of the same plant in case some do not survive the growing season. You can create additional plant Familiars from a primary plant set within a magical garden circle. There are two ways of accomplishing this task. If you have a plant already in the ground, gently dig down a few inches near the roots, place a quartz crystal, and bury it. Then around the plant, form a circle of eight quartz crystals. This should be done on the morning of the full moon.

To create a magical growing area that is currently void of plants, on the morning before the full moon form a ring of eight stones on the ground and place a quartz crystal about six inches deep in the soil, directly in the center of the circle. Then place a primary plant over the crystal and fill in the missing soil. Leave this in place overnight.

On the morning of the full moon, place a quartz crystal at each of the four quarters of this circle to mark the north, east, south, and west. The stones not marking the circle quarters may be quartz crystals or any assortment you choose, as long as they compliment each other. The spacing of the stones is determined by the physical needs of the plant and its growth. Therefore make sure you allow for enough room.

Method One

On the morning of the new moon remove the stones between the quarter crystals and plant a seed at each point. Next bury the quarter stones about an inch deep where they lay. The seeds should be of the same type as the plant within the circle. This will create additional "backup" Familiars, should anything happen to your original.

In order to establish a magical link with your potential Familiar you will need to pass energy into the soil where it grows, or will grow. Each day place both palms upon the ground within the circle and form a triangle with index fingers and thumbs touching. The stem of the plant should be in the open center of the triangle formed by your hands. Using your imagination and visualization, sense your power flowing out through your arms and into the crystal buried beneath the soil. The source of the power you are sending can be from one or more of your personal power centers.

As the plant grows, you must talk to it and mentally send visuals that communicate its occult properties. Make sure that you care well for the plant, watering, fertilizing, and protecting it from damage. To create a strong bond with your plant Familiar add three drops of your blood to a quart of water, using this mixture to water your plant as needed.

By performing the techniques I've described, you will have increased the power level of the numen through proximity to the crystal. Secondly, any other plants within the circle area will absorb the power and influence of the plant closest to the center crystal. This is because these plants grew under the influence of the center plant Familiar.

The final step in creating this plant Familiar is to establish your "linking" and rapport. To do this you must sit comfortably before the plant at the north quarter, facing south. Stare at the plant and allow your vision to slightly blur so that the plant goes out of focus. In this state observe the general shape of the plant. Let your mind be blank and keep your thoughts from intruding on the moment. At some point the plant will mentally send you an image of itself as a figure of some type. It will seem like a distorted image of the plant, but something suggestive of an animal, insect, or some other creature. Whatever shape is revealed to you will be the Familiar spirit contained within the plant.

The Familiar will give you extra power in any magical work whenever you summon it. House plants can become protective entities for your home through this technique. Plants given as gifts can be very useful for magical purposes as well. To summon your Familiar, you simply imagine your plant in its setting, and visualize it becoming the image of the spirit Familiar. Mentally draw it to yourself and allow it to merge within your thoughts. Experience the entity form, imagining that you are that creature. See yourself as the entity form, be the form, act like the form. This is how it becomes a "Familiar" spirit. Once you can perform this successfully, then you will possess a Familiar spirit.

Method Two

On the day of the new moon plant a seed over the buried crystal. Each day, after sunset, focus your power through your hands (as in method one). Your source of power must be drawn upon before you begin. When you are ready, sit comfortably before the plant, at the west quarter, facing east. Close your eyes and visualize the full moon above you. Mentally draw the moon down as a visual image until it sits just above your head. Next, visualize its light glowing brightly, then draw the moon down to your stomach area. Finally, visualize the moon expanding until it encloses you totally. The image would be similar seeing a person sitting inside a glowing white balloon.

At this point you will begin to pour the light out through your hands. You may drain the light out completely if you wish, or simply a portion of it, releasing the rest back into the air. In any case you must rid your body of the gathered power.

Now you can send your visual communications to the plant, establishing what is desired of the Familiar. This method works extremely well for the creation of magical plants as well. Create an "image play" for the plant, running through how you will use the plant Familiar, and showing it the successful outcome of the spell, potion, or whatever. In other words, you will be focusing and directing a "day dream" upon the plant. Include images of summoning the Familiar, and the work of the Familiar, in your visual communication. As in method one, you must take good care of the plant. You may add other plants to the stone circle with this method also if you desire. Talking to the plant is important, as it will aid in the bonding.

For Extra Potency

On the night before the moon is full perform the following: Set out an open jar of the water you will be using for the plant. Place it so that the moonlight falls directly upon the jar. If possible use a green glass jar or a green filter over the jar. Leave this out for the night and be sure to remove it before sunrise. On the night of the full moon, pour some of this water out upon the plant and around the circle. Then take some white flour and mark an X on the soil inside the circle, with the plant occupying the center of the X. The stones of the circle surround the X. If you desire you can set a crystal at each outside end of the X in order to enhance the power focused upon the plant.

By aligning the Familiar to the moon in this way, the technique will make the chemical properties of the plant more potent and it will increase its magical potential. Being attuned to lunar energy allows the plant to be more active within the astral and subconscious spheres of influence.

Working with Plant Familiars

In method one you were shown the technique for summoning the Familiar. Now we will look at some common shamanic techniques for using the Familiar.

Potions: In the case of herbal potions (or other liquids) you can charge them with the aid of your Familiar. Set the potion before you and summon the spirit Familiar. After you have successfully linked, mentally project the Familiar out into the potion. See it enter the potion, swimming and diving within the liquid. As it performs these acts, see the liquid begin to glow with a color that corresponds to the desired magical effect.

Incense: For powdered or herbal bulk incense, summon the Familiar and send it to rest upon the material. Mentally see it walk upon the surface, occasionally digging down into the material and reappearing through the surface. See the material begin to glow with the symbolic color of the desired magical effect, until it seems fully charged. Then recall the Familiar and return it to the plant.

Healing: Summon the plant Familiar and project it into the body of the person (or animal, etc.) concerned. First visualize it being the size of the patient, and see it merge with him or her. Mentally see the patient glowing with the symbolic color of the desired effect. If a specific area of the body is concerned, visualize the Familiar smaller in size and then focus the Familiar upon the area that requires healing. See the Familiar move in and out, removing and discarding the illness. This can be visualized as bits of dark material or whatever may seem appropriate. Intensify the magical color in this area for the healing. When the work has been completed, recall the Familiar and return it to the plant.

Amulets and Talismans: Plant Familiars can be used to add power to an amulet, seal, or talisman. To accomplish this, summon the Familiar and project it onto the object. Visualize it grasping onto the edges, and see the object glowing with the symbolic color of the desired effect. Carry the amulet or talisman with the Familiar attached to it. However, be sure to return the Familiar to the plant within a few days.

Minds: Familiars can be used to influence the thoughts and emotions of other people. Through your Familiar you can lend someone else some creativity, inspiration, motivation, or whatever. Normally, this is most effective when the person is asleep or under the influence of a drug, as in the case of major surgery. Even when the person is fully conscious, this method can still be effective.

Summon your Familiar and project it into the mind of the person desired. See it perched upon the crown of the head, then mentally have it enter through the "third eye" power center. Leave it within the person's mind while they sleep (or for several hours if the person is conscious) and then recall it, returning it to the plant. As always, you must instruct the Familiar mentally (or verbally) as to what it is to accomplish, and you must direct it during the work.

Magical Plants

The ancient Greek word for Witch was *pharmakis*, indicating one who possessed the knowledge of plant extracts. The Latin word for Witch was *venefica*, signifying one who knew the poisonous elements of plants, as well as one who practiced magic. The intimate knowledge of plants has been associated with Witches and Witchcraft for over 2,500 years. Many of the plants associated with Witchcraft are extremely poisonous and deadly, and should not be ingested or inhaled, nor allowed to come into contact with open wounds on the skin.

If you desire to work with plants as your Familiar image, then you will need to know the magical/mystical qualities of various plants associated with Witchcraft. These nonphysical properties can be conveyed into a sphere by creating thought-forms that contain the mental images of what the plant can accomplish. For example, a plant that has sedative abilities can be sent in a Familiar form to someone suffering from insomnia. A plant that has stimulating properties can be sent in Familiar form to someone who is in a rut or needs a renewal of creative energy.

In effect, the plant Familiar passes into the aura of the target and imparts its energy. The aura takes in the charge and the "image imprint" is incorporated into the aura. Once this takes place, then the thoughts and emotions of the individual are influenced by the intent of the magical charge.

In order to discover the occult nature of possible Familiar forms, let's look at some of the more traditional plants associated with Witchcraft. Their occult natures can be concentrated into nonphysical energy patterns directed into thought-forms that can be conveyed through your Familiar.

Belladonna (Atropa belladonna) is one of the oldest plants associated with Witchcraft. Its name means "the beautiful lady" and it is also known by the common name "deadly nightshade." Belladonna is native to southern and central Europe and has been cultivated in parts of England. Belladonna is poisonous and was used in small amounts to induce trance for astral projection and for producing altered states of consciousness in ritual and magical settings.

Hellebore (Helleborus niger) is a deadly plant, often used in ancient times to poison food. It is native to central and southern Europe, as well as Greece and Asia Minor. Hellebore is said to be effective against nervous disorders and hysteria. Its magical properties were said to render one invisible to others, and to possess the ability to break any spell.

Hemlock (Conium masculatum) is an extremely poisonous plant, once used in ancient Greece to execute criminals. It is native to most regions of Europe except the far north. Hemlock is a sedative and antispasmodic. The ancients believed it could counter madness, such as displayed in cases of hydrophobia. It has also been said to cure tumors and has been considered in cancer treatment.

Henbane (*Hyosycamus niger*) is one of the ancient plants associated with magic. It is native to southern and central Europe, but can frequently be found in England, Scotland, Wales, and even in Ireland. It is one of the primary ingredients allegedly used in the legendary Witches' flying ointment. In ancient mythology it was said that the dead received a crown of henbane leaves when they entered the Underworld. Henbane can be magically used to help the soul during the death experience, and to communicate with departed souls.

Foxglove (*Digitalis purpurea*) is one of the traditional magical plants associated with Witchcraft. It is native to almost all regions of continental Europe and the British Isles. Foxglove is associated with love spells, and is actually the source of the heart medicine known as digitalis. This plant is intimately connected with fairies in many European tales.

Mandrake (*Atropa mandragora*) is one of the best known of the magical plants associated with Witchcraft. Mandrake root was used in ancient times to induce trance states. It is native to southern Europe and was first cultivated in England by William Turner (1510–1568), who was known as the "father of British botany." English Mandrake (*Bryonia dioica*) is a plant commonly known as white bryony, and is a different species than classic mandrake. The root of the mandrake is large and woody and often resembles a human form. Therefore it was frequently used in poppet magic, and credited with power over the human body.

Wolfbane or *Monkshood* (*Aconite napellus*) is the deadliest of all the plants associated with Witchcraft. The name wolfbane (from the Greek *lycotonum*) arose from the practice of hunting wolves with arrows dipped in the juice of the aconite plant. Monkshood was originally indigenous to Eastern Europe but was grown in ancient Greece and spread to Italy. It is now found even in the western counties of England and in South Wales. Monkshood can produce profoundly altered states of consciousness, and was a favorite in shapeshifting magic.

Pennyroyal (*Mentha pulegium*) is a plant associated with magic and mystical virtues. Pennyroyal oil was used in ancient times as the base material for oils of initiation. Pennyroyal is native to most regions of Europe and parts of Asia. Occult legends attribute mystical insights and enlightenment to pennyroyal.

Rue (*Ruta graveolens*) is a plant associated with magic and protection since the days of ancient Etruria. Amulets shaped like rue were popular among the Etruscans, and the plant appears as a background design in many Etruscan paintings that depict gods, goddesses, and mythological themes. The Italian Witches' charm known as the *cimaruta*, which identifies one as a Witch, is a stylized sprig of rue bearing various symbols on the buds. While rue is widely attributed with protective powers, it is also said to unlock hidden realms, and bring one favor with the moon goddess.

Fennel (*Foeniculum vulgare*) is a plant associated with light and enlightenment. It is native to the Mediterranean but is found now throughout much of Europe. In an-cient myth, fire was stolen from the gods on a stalk of fennel. Ritual battles over the outcome of the harvest were fought with fennel and sorghum stalks. Here the fennel represented victory of the forces of light over darkness, of the waxing powers over the waning. Some occultists claim that fennel strengthens night vision, seeing hidden things.

Rosemary (*Rosemarinus officinalis*) is a plant associated with psychic ability, memory, mental clarity, and general well-being. It is native to the southern Europe. Rosemary is attributed with the protective powers, and is said to be influential in matters of love.

Vervain (*Verbena officinalis*) is a plant associated with the fairy race. It is native throughout much of Europe. Vervain is said to possess the power to banish evil spirits. It is also said to have healing powers over uncommon diseases.

Periwinkle (*Vinca major*) is a plant attributed with many magical properties. It was once known as the "sorcerer's violet" and in Italian Witchcraft it is called *centocchio* (the hundred eyes). In medieval texts periwinkle is reported as useful in the making of enchantments and love potions.

Primrose (*Primula vulgaris*) is a plant associated with initiation and magical paths in general. It is native to western Europe. The primrose has sedative properties and is said to invoke passion, joy, and euphoria.

For additional plants and their associated properties you can consult a good herbal book. See suggested reading list in the back of this book.

Part Two:
Magical Charges

There is a specific type of energy that many occultists call the *Odic* Force (pronounced Oh-dek). It is believed to be the underlying principle, or metaphysical nature, behind the physical forces of electricity and magnetism (as well as light and heat). In metaphysical terms Od (pronounced like the word owed) is the very fabric of the universe and is present in all things to varying degrees. Generally speaking, liquids, metals, and crystals are the best conductors as they easily absorb Odic energy and retain the original charge.

Oils are the preferred liquids to use with Odic charges because they do not evaporate as readily as water. This provides greater longevity for magical charges to remain active and in place. The Odic force is a very refined etheric substance. It can be controlled and directed by the power of the mind. Magical thought-forms can be bound to an Odic charge and placed within an object to establish a magical desire.

The Odic energy is essentially accumulated through deep breathing, which condenses the energy within the lungs. The Odic energy can then be informed with a desire through mental imagery and emotional intensity. The blood flowing through the lungs carries with it the electromagnetically charged imagery from centers within the brain. The blood in turn passes the charged imagery into the Odic energy accumulating in the lungs. In occult terms this is known as informing, which is the magical act of impregnating an object or substance with a concept (such as healing) embedded within an electromagnetic charge. Once the energy is accumulated and charged it can then be magically informed. See the section titled "Informing" for further details.

The Odic Breath

The technique is for accumulating Odic energy is very simple and can performed by following these basic steps:

1. Relax your body and allow your thoughts to become calm; still the mind.

2. Focus your attention upon the desire of your magical work. See its outcome clearly in your mind.

3. Rouse the emotions in order to charge the blood. Fill yourself with the desire for the outcome. If employing sexual stimulation as a power source, begin during this phase.

4. Begin deep breathing through the mouth only, taking in and releasing four breaths in succession while drawing in the stomach muscles slightly. This will keep air out of the stomach and help you to fill the lungs only.

5. Hold the breath on the next inhale and mentally transfer the image of your desire to the heart area/chakra.

6. Slowly release the breath out upon the object you wish to charge. As you do so, mentally transfer the image of the desire, seeing the image carried out upon the breath. Your desire is now magically transferred into the object and will vibrate with the energy of your desire—thus attracting it, like unto like.

Forming an Energy Sphere

To raise a sphere of power place your hands in front of you, about six inches apart (palms facing), and begin to move them slowly back and forth (like playing an accordion). Experience the sensations of warmth, pressure, and magnetism. Once a sphere of power has been established you can pass a mental sigil into it, or project a thought-form, thereby giving the sphere its purpose. Then mentally visualize the sphere entering the object that you wish to charge.

To increase this energy, use your concentration and imagination as you visualize a glowing force of power. Do not allow your hands to touch while performing this exercise. Once you have accomplished this method, then begin putting your hands around various objects and feeling their energy fields. Soon you will discover many other uses for this basic ability.

Informing

In chapter three we touched briefly on the topic of informing, and we will consider it in more depth and in a slightly different context. Informing is the art of transferring mental images, through the willpower of the mind, into target objects or substances. As human beings we all possess the creative spark of that which created us. Therefore, on a lesser scale we too can create by drawing upon the indwelling spiritual essence of our own being. All that is required is to bring one's will under control, and to employ it to build crystal clear images. Added to this is the energy of burning desire to empower the image and transfer it.

The most effective method to stimulate the breath is to employ sexual stimulation. It is through such stimulation that the power centers of the body open in response, flooding the central nervous system and stimulating the endocrine glands. The blood becomes electromagnetically charged by the metaphysical heat created by the stimulation and quickened breathing. The essence of this charge is carried in the vapor emitted from the lungs, the breath of magic. Many ancient magical texts employ the breath in spell casting and other works of magic.

Once the blood is magically heated, then the mind infuses it with a mental image symbolizing the desired effect. This image is essential to binding the magical charge so that it can be transmitted upon the breath. The charge must be allowed to build within the blood until you feel a sensation of internal heat and pulsating blood. Once this point has been reached, then the breath may be directed out toward the talisman that will contain it, or toward the target you wish to influence. To successfully wield energy you must be able to concentrate and project (fix and direct) with the power of your mind/will.

Thought-Form Familiars

A thought-form is a mental image created by the mind. It is given substance within the etheric astral material and is animated by the indwelling consciousness of whatever is invoked within it. This is the metaphysical basis of the magical servant or Witches' Familiar. Basically, thought-forms are built up by a combination of raised energy from the physical body and mental images from the mind (concentration/visualization).

The thought-form must be routinely fed energy in order to continue its existence in the early stages of its creation. The danger here is that should the form not receive energy from its creator then it may draw it from another source upon the planes. This is undesirable because it may become possessed by a consciousness dwelling upon the planes (or an earth-bound spirit) or it may become a type of incubus or succubus. In the latter case it will draw energy from its creator and may cause severe fatigue or even illness. Therefore when a thought-form is created it should be performed in a manner that will determine the length of its existence and the method of its termination.

Through the creation of thought-forms a person can transmit influences, establish temporary protection around a place, object, or person, and generally create a useful servant on the mental or astral plane (the spheres of influence). The basic procedure for creating a simple thought-form is as follows:

1. Make or obtain a statue or image that corresponds to the nature you wish your thought-form to possess (for example, a wolf for protection). Hollow out the statue and fill it with sand or liquid. As an alternative you can place a small vial of liquid within the base of the statue.

2. Place the statue in front of you and sit in a comfortable position. Then visualize a sphere of light above your head. The color of the light must be symbolic of the nature of your desired effect.

3. Mentally draw the light down into your head and bring it to rest directly between your eyebrows. Concentrate strongly upon the statue and its nature. Use the Odic breath and informing technique described in this chapter to empower the thought-form.

4. Now give the thought-form a name that is appropriate to the work it will perform for you. Say out loud: "I name thee _____."

5. Verbally instruct the thought-form, telling it when to work (time of day and night), where to work, how long, and when to finish. Then instruct it to terminate its existence on a given day and time. Do not extend the existence of the thought-form beyond seven days.

6. Release the thought-form, instructing it to go forth. Tell it to return to the statue when it requires more energy, and when it is not working as instructed. Each day you will want to feed the thought-form by putting energy into the statue (see Odic breath).

7. When the time has come to terminate the thought-form, slowly drain the liquid or sand out of the statue into a hole dug in the earth. As you empty the statue, feel the thought-form dissolve and ebb away. Finally, verbally affirm that the connection is now severed and the thought-form is dissolved. This step is vital; do not omit it.

Now that we have looked at the different types of Familiars and learned something of the benefits and drawbacks, it is time to learn how to return the Familiar spirit to the place of its origin. In the next chapter we will discuss how to part with a Familiar.

5

Parting with the Familiar

The day will undoubtedly come when you and your familiar will part ways. In the case of a physical Familiar, death will eventually occur and you will most likely want to free the animal's spirit to move on to the spirit world. It is not uncommon for loyal Familiars to "take a magical hit" in place of their human partner. This can often lead to disease or death for the animal. You will want to take that into consideration before deciding on having a physical Familiar.

In the case of an artificial elemental, its existence is quite temporary at best, and must be dissolved within a few days in any case. Even the spirit or astral elemental cannot be allowed to stay in the physical realm for long extended periods of time. The spirit or astral Familiar can quickly rejuvenate from any magical hits it might receive.

There are certain risks and dangers involved when working with Familiars. The bonds and connections run deep and encompass the mind, body, and spirit. It is not a relationship to enter into lightly. Parting with the physical/pet Familiar due to the death of the animal is difficult and emotionally painful. Coming to the end of your relationship with an astral/spirit Familiar impacts not only the emotions but extends to the aura and spirit housed in your physical body. Therefore caution must be used in all dealings with Familiar spirits.

Before exploring the various techniques and rites associated with releasing a Familiar, it is advisable to discuss the occult concepts behind the reasons for releasing and severing one's connection to Familiar. These include teachings concerning the aura, astral beings, and personal energy centers. It will also be helpful to understand the mechanism of magnetism and attachment. In this way you can be better prepared to deal with problems, and learn how to avoid them in the first place.

Part One:
The Energy Bodies

In our human condition we are comprised of mind, spirit, and body. From an occult perspective the body is divided into two vessels, the flesh vehicle and the astral double. So in effect we have four aspects: mind, body, astral body, and spirit. Occult tradition also states that there are four worlds: spiritual, mental, astral, and physical.

Each of the bodies is attuned to one of the four planes, and shares an elemental relationship to the planes as well (see fig. 15, p. 104). The interaction between the four bodies creates an energy field called the aura. The aura often appears as a large oval sphere surrounding the physical body, and extends outward to approximately the distance of a full arm extension in any direction. Anything at this distance or closer causes an energy reaction of varying degrees within the aura.

In Western occultism there are three bands comprising the aura. In Eastern mysticism there are seven bands. The Western system incorporates the magnetic aura, astral aura, and spiritual aura. The Eastern system includes the health, emotional, mental, psychic, causal, spiritual, and cosmic universal bands. For the purposes of this chapter we will focus on the Western system of three auric bands.

1. The magnetic band of the aura lies closest to the physical body and reflects the health of the material form. In some occult organizations the magnetic band is also known as the etheric band. The energy of the magnetic band maintains cohesion, establishing order and balance within the material form, which houses the soul. Due to its cohesive nature the magnetic band can pick up unwanted "etheric parasites" that may come into contact with it during the types of magical work required for using the nonphysical Familiar.

   Etheric parasites, and magical work involving portals to and from this dimension, can cause "auric wounds" that allow vital energy to bleed off from the aura. This can cause the affected person to feel a loss of energy to experience a lack of drive in daily life.

   At least once a month it is a good idea to cleanse and recharge your aura in order to rid yourself of any unwelcome entities that may have attached themselves to your etheric body. To accomplish this requires bathing in sunlight for twenty to thirty minutes along with an energy "scrubbing," using some clean water and a fresh pine branch (needles intact). After soaking up the sunlight, dip the pine branch in the water and run it across your skin, head to toe, front and back. Do one section of the body at a time, shake the branch off, and then

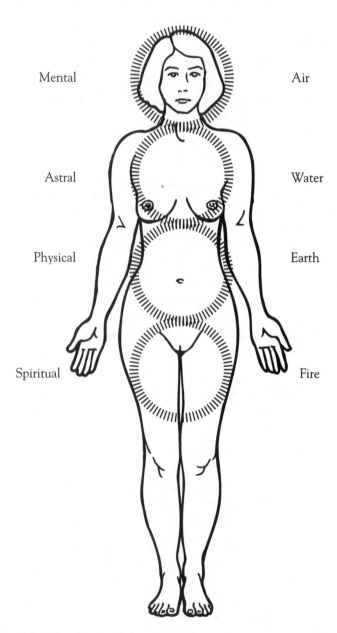

Mental

Astral

Physical

Spiritual

Air

Water

Earth

Fire

Fig. 15: The Aura and Associations

dip it in the water and repeat the process. It is best to be
unclothed when performing this technique.

Once the aura has been cleansed it is time to rejuvenate or recharge it. Find an evergreen tree in a place
where you will be undisturbed for at least a half hour.
To approach the tree, extend your open palms toward
the tree and close your eyes. Try and sense the indwelling spirit of the tree as a sentient being. When you feel
a connection then sit with your back against the tree.

Focus your mind upon the tree as a separate being,
and try to mentally communicate a sense of kindred-
ness. Try to sense it sending you the same feelings.
Next allow yourself to sink back into the tree as you
might into a friend or lover sitting cuddled up behind
you. Then separately take in three slow deep breaths,
exhaling fully outward with each one.

At this phase place your palms down on the ground
beside you. Press your tailbone firmly but gently against
the ground. Imagine now that you are part of the earth
beneath you, as well as part of the tree and the air around
you. Press down lightly but firmly on the ground with
the palms of your hands. Mentally extend yourself into
your surrounding. Imagine that you are rooted in the
center of it all, very much like the tree is rooted in the
spot where you sit.

Practice this a few times until you can sense yourself
being rejuvenated by Nature each time you perform the
technique. Before long you will realize that this is pre-
cisely what is taking place. Once you embrace the reality that you are not separate from Nature, and that you
and the tree, the air, and the soil are all equal, then
Nature will pour into your very center and renew your
vitality. It will share with you what it shares with everything actively connected to it.

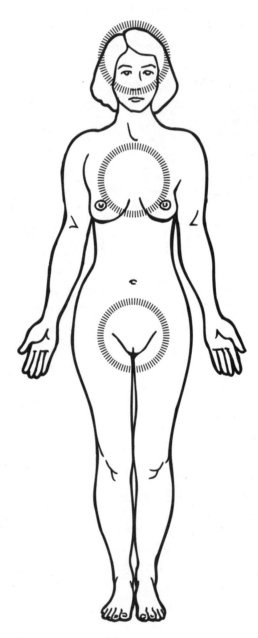

Fig. 16a: The Primary Chakra Centers

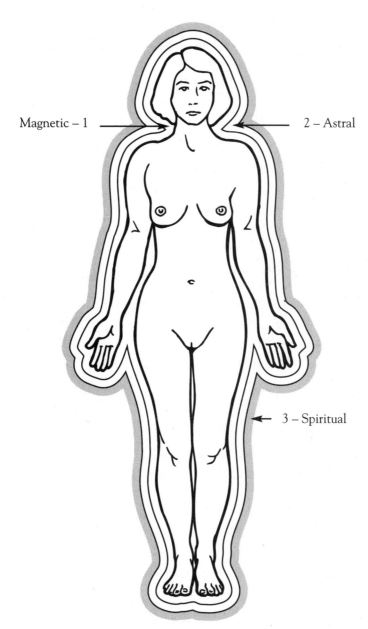

Magnetic – 1

2 – Astral

3 – Spiritual

Fig. 16b: The Aura Bands

2. The astral aura band manifests next to the magnetic aura, and within its material appears what is known as the chakra or personal power centers (see fig. 16b, p. 107). These centers vitalize the aura and work together to generate vitality and occult power.

Since the astral band envelops the magnetic band, it can be fortified to serve as a shield against random attachment to the magnetic aura.

Occult teachings indicate that the chakra centers (see fig. 16a, p. 106) are vitalized by the rays of the sun. It is the etheric counterpart of sunlight that nurtures the aura bands and the energy centers. According to the teachings, the solar plexus of the material body is the gateway for receiving this energy. In order to vitalize the chakra emanations into the aura you can perform the Elemental Centering technique.

Stand with your legs together, arms resting at your side, and the palms of your hands facing forward (see fig. 17). Visualize a sphere of bright light above your head. Say the following words and then mentally draw the sphere down into your forehead area, visualizing a white glowing light:

I call upon Spirit, the source of all things.

Then mentally move the sphere down to your neck area, visualize a glowing blue light, and say:

By the power of Spirit over the four elements,
I invoke air.

Next, mentally move the sphere down to your heart area, visualize a glowing green light, and say:

By the power of Spirit over the four elements,
I invoke water.

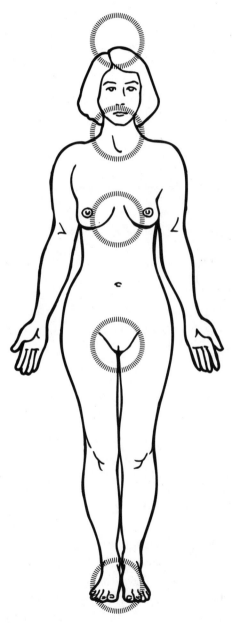

Fig. 17: The Elemental Charge

Now, mentally move the sphere down to your genital area, visualize a glowing red light, and say:

By the power of Spirit over the four elements,
I invoke fire.

Finally, mentally move the sphere down to your feet, visualize a glowing yellow light, and say:

By the power of Spirit over the four elements,
I invoke earth.

After a few moments, visualize all of the centers moving (one by one) into the area of your navel. Then visualize this area glowing white, and say:

By Spirit joined with the four elements,
This charge I give . . .

At this phase visualize the sphere expanding outward from the navel and enveloping you completely (head to toe) in a glowing oval sphere. After this image is clearly established, then say these words:

By the power of Spirit over the four elements,
By the power of spirit joined with the four
*   elements,*
I invoke now the quintessence:
As above, so below, as within, so without.

The Elemental Centering technique not only creates an intensified aura field but can also be used for magical purposes and personal shielding of the aura bands. Because you are incorporating the four elements into your aura, this establishes the essential components of creativity that are essential to magic. Therefore you can then create energy spheres and pass thought-forms into them that will be much more potent.

3. The spiritual aura band manifests as the outermost layer
   of auric bands. The spiritual band connects a person to
   his or her higher self, where one meets with the cosmic
   forces. From an occult perspective humans are comprised of three distinct selves, the lower, middle, and
   higher self.

   The lower self is the instinctual and primal self, the
   material nature. The middle self is the mental self where
   personal image and ego manifest. The higher self is the
   merging of one's consciousness with the divine, the
   sacred nature of the soul. What becomes established
   in the higher self passes down into the middle and lower
   selves where reflected elements of this state of consciousness then manifest.

   A technique exists that is designed to create a thought-
   form in the outer auric band, which will establish a
   temporary "high order" image in the entire auric field.
   When established, this image provides the person with
   significant magical abilities that can be used for protection, banishing, or dissolving. Occultists often refer to
   this as the magical personality.

   In order to create a magical personality, it is necessary to mentally establish it through meditation that is
   focused upon the Triad of Power: *Wisdom, Compassion,*
   and *Power.* To safely wield the power available to the
   higher self (for yourself and those around you) such
   power must be balanced by compassion and governed
   by wisdom.

   To establish the magical personality within the aura,
   begin by selecting a new and unused ring or amulet.
   Choose one that strongly symbolizes magical power to
   you. For the Witch this is often the pentagram. You will
   then need to take on a magical name for the magical
   persona. The name can be anything that appeals to

you and suggests a higher nature than your mundane personality.

Next you will need to meditate on each of the three natures: wisdom, compassion, and power. Spend some time mentally focusing on each one, exploring what they mean to you. It may be helpful to consult a dictionary for precise meanings, and then look further into the etymology of each word.

When you are ready to begin, stand with your feet together, arms resting at your sides, with the palms facing outward (fig. 18). Beginning with the concept of power, picture in your mind's eye the precise power you wish to wield. Create within your mind a "daydream" scenario in which you possess and use this power according to your desire. Then fix the image in your mind with a "still frame" picture that best symbolizes this power. When you picture this clearly, then say the following words:

> *I call upon Spirit over the four elements to invoke within me this power of magic through which I can manifest my desire in accordance with my will.*

Next, focus your mind on the nature of compassion. Create within your mind a "daydream" scenario in which you exercise compassion toward those in proximity of your power. Fix a still-frame image in your mind that best symbolizes this compassion. When you picture this clearly, then say the following words:

> *I call upon Spirit over the four elements to instill within me the compassion that is my higher nature, through which my magic shall be in balance.*

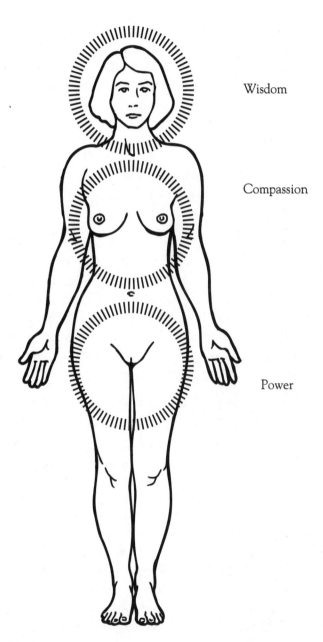

Wisdom

Compassion

Power

Fig. 18: The Empowerment Charge

Finally, focus your mind on the nature of wisdom. As before, create within your mind a daydream in which you possess the wisdom required to responsibly wield power that may affect others. Fix a "still frame" image in your mind that best symbolizes this state of wisdom. When you have pictured this clearly, then say the following words:

I call upon Spirit over the four elements to instill within me the wisdom of the Higher Self, through which I accomplish my desire, and against whose light, no evil thing may prevail.

Remaining in the ritual posture, begin to visualize a silvery mist forming behind you. Mentally bring the image to appear as a hooded, robed figure, exactly your size, standing directly behind you. Once this image is clear in your mind, then put on the ring or amulet. As you do so, mentally see the robed figure merge into your body. Once this is firm in your mind, say the following words of affirmation and alignment:

I am (magical name) *born of power, compassion and wisdom. Though here in world, my race is of the stars. I am the bearer of the divine light of the Higher Self, and in my presence may no evil thing remain.*

In this enhanced state of consciousness you can perform any magical acts that are necessary. You can cleanse an area and banish any unwanted spirits or etheric parasites. You can also take control over unwelcome or errant Familiars and undo any magical situation that has gone astray.

When you are finished, it is vital that you perform the following technique for releasing. To accomplish this, visualize the silver mist forming once again behind you. Slowly begin to slip off the ring or amulet. As you do, visualize the robed figure separating from you and being dissolved back into the mist.

As the ring leaves your finger, or the amulet lifts off over your head, mentally see the figure disappear completely into the mist. Then visualize the mist fading away. Look all around you and confirm that everything is normal in your surroundings.

Whenever you need to invoke this presence again, stand in the posture, visualize the silver mist and then speak each of the invocations for power, compassion, and wisdom as you did before (you do not need to repeat the daydream visualizations). Then put on the ring or amulet, and visualize the robed figure merging with you from the mist. Always make sure to release it each time once you have finished. For an expanded use of the magical personality see my book *Wiccan Magick*.

Astral Doorways

It is an ancient occult teaching that a realm exists just beyond our material world. It has been called by many names such as the Otherworld, Spirit World, and even the Fairy Realm. Some people imagine that this world is separated from the material one by a door, gate, or a veil. It is a common expression among many modern Witches that the "veil grows thin" at the time of Samhain or All Hallow's Eve.

Whenever the elemental spirits are called upon for magic or ritual, the elemental plane is stimulated. The elemental plane can be pictured as a river flowing to and from the material world and the astral realm. When it is activated, from either end, energy flows to the gateway.

If this energy is of a certain resonance it can open the portal and pass into the next world. This is a natural process and is also the means by which many forms of magic manifest the desired goal. Unfortunately whenever the portals to and from the world open, various entities can take the opportunity to slip through. This is one of the reasons why Witches establish protections around their ritual circles when working magic or performing seasonal rites.

When working with entities that pass through astral doorways, it becomes easier for them to do so, even when not summoned if their presence is clearly unwanted. In such cases you will need a symbol of power to deter them. The pentagram is an effective symbol for Witches because it sigilizes the power of spirit over the four elements of earth, air, fire, and water. It should always be worn when working with astral energy and/or summoning the Familiar from the next dimension. In effect, the pentagram depicts the ancient mythos of Spirit taming chaos.

Many myths of the ancient world speak of chaos existing in the dark formless universe long before the world was created. Such myths tell us that Spirit (the gods) drew the four creative elements of earth, air, fire, and water from out of chaos and bound them together. With the four elements brought into balance and harmony by the presence of spirit, the worlds were then able to form into functional realms.

When spirits of other realms view the pentagram it represents to them the power to establish order, bind, and create a reality in accordance with the will of the one who bears/wears the pentagram. Spirits react to the principle made manifest, much like we react when speeding done the road and seeing the markings of the police department on the vehicle next to us. We become compliant to the power behind the symbol. Always remember that to an astral being thoughts are things.

Astral doorways can be sealed closed whenever you feel the need. To accomplish this, face east and visualize a door being closed tight before you. Then use your athame and trace a large X in the air. While tracing the X, say these words:

> By the powers of the sacred blade,
> I seal the door and bar the way.

Repeat the entire process facing west. Then trace a circle in the air (east and then west as before) and trace a five-pointed star within it. As you do, say these words:

> By spirit over earth, air, water, and fire,
> here none may enter against my desire.

If you seal a doorway in this way, then you will need to open it later when you wish to summon. To do this hold your arms crossed at the wrists in front of you, palms facing you at eye level. Turn to the east and visualize a door with an X on it, as though two wooden planks had been nailed across the doorway. Then speak the following words, and immediately upon completion, you must quickly and firmly pull your arms away from one another, jetting each one off to the opposite side:

> By spirit over the elements, here on this day
> I unseal the door and open the way.

Repeat the process at the west quarter.

Etheric Parasites

In the material world there are various creatures that live off a host creature. These parasites are part of the natural order. In the astral realm such creatures also exist and function according to the laws of that reality. This is, in part, an aspect of the occult teaching that states "That which is above, is as that which is below, and that which is below, is as that which is above."

This means that the mechanism of one reflects or mirrors that of another, but because the nature of each plane differs from the other, the reflection is somewhat distorted or re-interpreted in accord with the essential nature of any given plane. An example is that a tree appears solid and stationary within the material world, but on the astral plane is a fluid energy pattern. On the material plane a tree is the lowest or most base manifestation of the entity that is the tree on the spiritual plane.

As mentioned in the previous section, various entities may slip through an open portal whenever you perform any work designed to summon from outside the material realm. In addition, earthbound entities may also be attracted to a magical work of summoning. As noted earlier, part of the aura is magnetic in nature and there is a natural tendency to draw things toward it.

The exercises in this chapter will help create an energy shield around the magnetic aura, which will make it difficult for parasitic entities to attach themselves. On a mundane level these entities mean no intentional harm, anymore than does a flea or a tick. It is simply their nature to *feed* upon other creatures. In reality we all do this, even vegetarians. Life is life, no matter what container it dwells in.

In addition to the techniques provided in this chapter, you can also help rid yourself of parasitic entities (and negative thought-forms) through such mundane acts as taking a shower. All that is required is an affirmation and a visualization. While taking a shower, lather with soup and verbally state that you are cleansing yourself of all negativity and anything attached to your mind, body, or spirit that is draining you of energy, vitality, and health.

As the lather rinses off your body and down the drain, visualize all negativity, illness, and contamination being carried away with it as it disappears down the drain. Verbally affirm that you are cleansed and freed. This also a good technique to use in order to rid yourself of negative feelings about another person.

Using the smoke from burning sage or Dragon's Blood incense is another method of cleansing one's aura, as well as cleansing your home in general, and bedroom specifically. It is best to open windows and pass the smoke from the back of the house/room and out a window or doorway. For personal cleansing of the aura you can start at the feet and work your way up to the top your head. Then make a spiral motion upward in a counterclockwise fashion, away from your head. Do this outdoors or near an open door or window. While performing this task, verbally affirm that you are cleansing and ridding yourself of all that is negative, evil, and unbalanced.

The Astral Substance

There is an occult saying that states "Thoughts are things." This saying refers to energy and the astral substance. In the astral realm the astral material itself forms around any energy that stimulates it. One way to imagine this is to picture soft clay having the ability to become whatever you portray in your mind. In other words, if you pictured a horse then the clay would form itself into the image of a horse. I've over-simplified this concept for the purpose of illustration, but I think it gives you a good idea of the basic inner mechanics of the astral realm.

When creating nonphysical Familiars such as the artificial Familiar you will be using magic to generate a form within the astral substance. Just as your physical body *houses* your soul, so too may an entity reside within an astral form of your creation. For this reason you must use caution and monitor the situation. Even though you may return the Familiar to the astral realm when not in use, the etheric bond between human and Familiar still allows for connection and communication. The only way to prevent this is to magically dissolve the relationship.

When you decide to release your Familiar and dissolve the bonds you will need to perform the Ritual of Dissolving, which is provided in part two of this chapter. Following this you will need to burn or bury everything associated with the Familiar. This will include any statue used to house the Familiar, as well as any special oil you used or charm/amulet you wore for connection.

If you leave anything intact within the physical dimension that had a magical or ritual connection to your Familiar, it is possible that the astral form may re-assemble from the energy connected to the item.

Part Two

Now that we have exposed some of the dangers related to working with Otherworld entities, and the necessary precautions, we can now look at the rituals for parting with a Familiar. A formal ritual will help you gain closure regarding the loss of a Familiar.

In effect, rites of release begin a process of accepting the loss that one is experiencing. Such rites also set into motion forces that allow the entity to move on away from the material world. We know from anthropological studies that ancient humans placed personal items in the graves of fellow tribal members. Some commentators believe that such an act indicated a belief in another life to follow. In addition it may also indicate a caring relationship, a well-wishing in preparation for the journey ahead.

The following rituals are designed to incorporate both the common and occult elements of releasing as found in many funeral rites. This material provides a basic format or structure, and I would encourage the reader to made additions and modifications that will personalize the rituals. Any ritual of release is as much for those left behind as it is for those who move on into the Otherworld.

Crossing-over Ritual

This ritual is designed to release a pet Familiar that has died. The altar should be oriented so that you look west when you face it during the ceremony. The candles should be placed to form a triangle, with one tip of the triangle pointing west. Set the altar with a black cloth and three red candles. Black is the color of the Underworld, the realm in which all things are renewed. Red is the color of life and passion, the vital essence of continuation. The triangle represents manifestation, and the point indicates the direction or focal point. The west is the doorway to the Otherworld.

On the west section of the altar place some incense of your choosing and something to contain it. Inside the triangle area on the altar place a photo or image of your pet Familiar. Also set a small bell on the altar. Place objects that your Familiar liked to play with anywhere on the altar. The objects can be anything such as a ball, a squeaky toy, or a stuffed animal. These items will later be buried with your pet or cremated in accordance with how you wish to take care of the physical remains.

To prepare for releasing your Familiar you can use the Seal of Departing (see chapter two). Place the seal lying down in front of the image or photo of your pet. With everything in place, you are ready to begin your ceremony of release. The following ceremony is for a dog, and you can modify the wording to suit the nature of your own pet. Therefore this ceremony will serve as a template for you to construct your own customized ritual:

1. Light the candles and incense.

2. Ring the bell.

3. Recite:

> With this ritual of release I bid farewell to you
> (name). I will remember the times we had

*together and the love we shared. Go now to the
Summerland and run free where fields, and hills,
and ponds await. Playful companions await you,
and your days will be happy and carefree.*

4. Blow some of the smoke toward the west quarter, or use
a feather to fan the fan in that direction. Visualize your
pet Familiar happily moving off through the west portal.

5. Pick up each pet toy, separately, and blow or fan some
incense smoke across it (facing west). Visualize an astral
image of the toy crossing over through the west portal.
Through this you are transferring an astral replica of
each toy to the Summerland.

6. Close the ritual with a prayer for the well being of your
pet.

7. All that is left to do now is to bury the toys from the
altar in the ground where they can remain undisturbed.
You can bury the pet with them or cremate it. You can
also burn the toys as a release if you wish.

Ritual for Dissolving

The purpose of this ritual is to sever psychic and astral connections related to the Familiar. To accomplish this you will need a
formal ritual setting in which you state and affirm the dissolving
of your connection to a Familiar.

Required items:
Salt
Small cauldron or metal bowl for burning.
1 self-igniting charcoal block (specifically made for incense)
4 garlic cloves
4 small dishes
4 black votive candles

2 black altar candles
1 red votive candle
Familiar spirit image/figure
Material links to Familiar
Seal of Departing (and other seals you wish to dissolve)

1. Using coarse salt, pour a circle of salt on the ground/
   floor large enough to sit in comfortably with a small
   altar set before you.

2. Place some crushed garlic cloves in a dish at each of the
   four quarters of the circle. In each dish also set a small
   black votive candle.

3. On your altar place a small cauldron or burning bowl in
   the center. Place a charcoal block inside the cauldron/
   bowl and light it. Then set a black votive candle in front
   of the cauldron.

4. In front of the votive candle place any seals you wish
   to dissolve ties with, and any physical objects once connected to or associated with your Familiar.

5. Light all the candles at each quarter. Then light the
   votive candle on the altar, as well as the altar candles
   themselves.

6. Sit in front of the altar and look at the black votive
   candle burning in front of you. Point at the seals and
   then at the Familiar images/connections, and recite
   these words as you hold the palms of your hands outward facing the altar:

> *To the south, west, north, and east*
> *by all my magic do I release*
> *that which my will once did yearn,*
> *what I created here I now return.*

7. Pick up each seal you wish to sever, and drop the seal
   in the cauldron/bowl. If using more than one seal burn
   each one separately. Watch the fire consume the seal,
   and visualize the energy being dissipated out to the four
   winds. If you made your seal out of soft clay instead of
   paper, then knead the clay to remove the symbolism.
   Light some paper in the cauldron/bowl and quickly pass
   the clay through the flames three times.

8. Using the Seal of Departing, study its symbolism for a
   few moments, hold it out in front of you, and then recite these words:

   > *Carry these forces to the four winds*
   > *And all ebb away through widdershins.*
   > *By air, earth, water, and fire,*
   > *I declare this done as I desire.*

You can enhance this by pointing a wand at the seal and making counterclockwise spiral movements with it as you recite the
incantation. Burning some Dragon's Blood incense is also an effective addition.

Once you have completed the ritual then you must dispose of
the debris. It is best to bury the candles, melted wax, ashes, and
other remnants in the soil. Pick a place where you will not have
to walk over the spot again. This will help ensure that no recon-
nection will take place accidentally. It is best to also bury any images, figurines, or statues that you used to create a bond with
your Familiar, or any that served in a magical setting.

The Vortex Ritual

The Vortex ritual is designed to immediately void all that you
created in connection with your Familiar. It is used in place of
the Seal of Departing or the Seal of Severance when the situation is an emergency and quick action that packs an extra punch

is required. This ritual should not be used unless things are really out of hand and you are fearful. This is because it requires destruction of the Genesis Seal without first releasing the Familiar, which will cause quite a magical jolt to the Familiar, forcefully tearing it away and propelling it out of this realm.

Required items:
Salt
Small cauldron or metal bowl for burning.
1 self-igniting charcoal block (specifically made for incense)
4 garlic cloves
4 small dishes
4 cups
4 ounces of vinegar
4 black votive candles
2 black altar candles
1 red votive candle
Familiar spirit image/figure
Material links to Familiar
Vortex Seal
All magic seals

1. Using coarse salt, pour a circle of salt on the ground/floor large enough to sit in comfortably with a small altar set before you.

2. Place some crushed garlic cloves in a dish at each of the four quarters of the circle. In each dish also set a small black votive candle. Next to each quarter votive candle place a cup containing one ounce of vinegar.

3. On the center of your altar place a small cauldron or burning bowl. Place a charcoal block inside the cauldron/bowl and light it. Then set a black votive candle in front of the cauldron.

4. In front of the votive candle place all of the magical seals (including the Genesis Seal) and any physical objects once connected to or associated with your Familiar.

5. Light all the candles at each quarter. Then light the votive candle on the altar, and the two altar candles.

6. Sit in front of the altar and look at the black votive candle burning in front of you. Point at the seals and then at the Familiar images/connections, and recite these words as you hold the palms of your hands outward facing the altar:

> *To the south, west, north, and east*
> *By all my magic do I release*
> *That which my will once did yearn,*
> *What I created here I now return.*

7. Pick up all of the seals (except the vortex seal) and drop them into the cauldron/bowl. Watch the fire consume the seals, and visualize the energy being dissipated out to the four winds. If you made your seal out of soft clay instead of paper, then knead the clay to remove the symbolism. Light some paper in the cauldron/bowl and quickly pass the clay through the flames three times.

8. Using the Vortex Seal, study its symbolism for a few moments, then set it in plain view in front of the cauldron before you on the altar. With your left hand, point your index finger directly at the flame and recite these words:

> *Sigil, form, and will's desire,*
> *Dissolve away in magic fire,*
> *All spirits of seals are drawn to you,*
> *And pass away from this world's view.*

Place the palms of both hands out facing the cauldron/bowl, and recite:

By the Lady—may moonlight join with sacred
Flame, and undo by magic all that I made.

As with the ritual of releasing you can also enhance this rite by pointing a wand at the vortex seal and making counterclockwise spiral movements as you recite the last verse of the incantation. Burning some Dragon's Blood incense will help banish any lingering spirits and will cleanse the setting.

As with all rituals, once you have completed the steps then you must dispose of the debris. All candles, melted wax, ashes, and other remnants must be buried in the ground where you will not have to walk over the spot again. This includes any images, figurines, or statues that you used to create a bond with your Familiar, or any that served in a magical setting.

Parting Words

Now we have come to the end of this book. At this point you should be aware of the seriousness of working intimately with Familiar spirits. In addition, the benefits of working with Familiars should also be evident. Reflect upon what you have read in this book, and then decide upon your course of action.

Working with occult forces draws energy into your aura and your chakra centers. Such energy tends to intensify various elements within the receiver. Dealing with occult energy will bring out your strengths and weaknesses. It is not unlike inflating a tire—if any weaknesses in the material exist, a bulge will develop. Occult energy stimulates the subconscious mind, and emotional or mental problems can become more profound. Therefore it is important that you perform the exercises provided in this chapter. Doing so will help you maintain an inner balance.

I also recommend that you keep a journal of your work with Familiar spirits. Review the journal at the end of each month and note any challenges, concerns, or problems. This will keep you from automatically adjusting to difficulties that you might eventually come to regard as normal. Always bear in mind that a healthy relationship never exceeds a 50/50 investment.

Always trust your instincts, intuition, and first thoughts when working with Familiars. Never do anything, or allow anything to take place, that frightens you. Fear is an energy, and it is one that you want to avoid. This is because this type of energy is very potent (just like anger is) and can provide a Familiar with more "power" than you may want it to be able to draw upon.

Until you gain more experience, you may wish to work with artificial elemental Familiars before calling upon Familiar spirits from the Otherworld. You can also work with a physical Familiar in the beginning. Even later on, it may serve you to keep a physical cat Familiar, which will help you keep an eye on things when other entities come into play. Once you feel confident, and are more comfortable with the experience in general, then you can move on to move to work with other types of entities.

Remember always that you are the Witch. This means that you are in control of the situation and the outcome. A Witch is never a victim; a Witch is a full participant in the affairs of his or her life. In closing, please be safe, be well, and keep things Familiar.

Appendix 1

Keyword Associations for Familiars

The following keywords indicate various associations that are connected to a diverse variety of animals and creatures. From an occult perspective, when a Familiar presents itself the keyword is then an indication of the gift, power, or ability it wishes you to have. Therefore the list provided here will serve as a quick reference guide.

On a mystical level the keywords associated with your Familiar may also be messages to you that address something in your current life experience. Whenever you face a challenge or feel you need direction, observe which animals present themselves to you. In this way we are all "spirit led" in troubled times and situations.

Mammals

Badger: self-reliance, tenacity, courage.

Bat: transition, initiation, detection.

Bear: power, endurance, strength, fearless.

Bobcat: silence, secrecy, solitary.

Cat (domestic): tenacity, patience, independence, mystery.

Coyote: wisdom, cleverness, trickster.

Deer: gentleness, innocence, agility.

Dog: faithfulness, protection.

Ferret: stealthiness, solitary.

Fox: cunning, clever, quickness.

Goat: fertility, determination, singlemindedness.

Hare: fertility, rebirth, intuition.

Horse: freedom, raw power.

Lynx: vision of the hidden and unseen.

Mouse: meticulous, fastidious.

Otter: joy, playfulness, sharing.

Porcupine: defense, preparedness.

Panther: beauty, gracefulness, quickness.

Raccoon: curiosity, dexterity.

Tiger: passion, power.

Weasel: slyness.

Wolf: guardianship, intuition.

Birds

Blue Jay: assertiveness.

Crow: opportunity, cleverness.

Eagle: nobility, strength.

Hawk: messenger, ally.

Hummingbird: agility, independence.

Mocking Bird: tenacity, manipulation, misdirection.

Owl: wisdom, contemplation.

Raven: secret knowledge, guardianship, mystical teachings.
Roadrunner: agility, speed.
Rooster: guardianship, vigilance, protection.
Vulture: purification, rebirth, guardianship.
Woodpecker: perseverance.
Wren: resourcefulness.

Reptiles

Frog: metamorphosis.
Lizard: focus, concentration.
Snake: initiation, rebirth, enlightenment.
Toad: prophecy, root strengths.
Turtle: longevity, tranquility, insulation, isolation.

Insects

Bee: cooperation, community, fellowship.
Beetle: rebirth, renewal through decomposition, resurrection.
Butterfly: transformation, freedom, beauty.
Dragonfly: metamorphosis, new perspectives, changes.
Spider: heighten senses, weaving patterns, patience.

Appendix 2

Concerning
Classic Familiars

This section provides some literary sources and historical Witch trial documentation regarding various animals associated with Witchcraft. This material demonstrates the deep roots of pre-Christian European religion that fed popular Witch lore well into the Renaissance period. Included also are references in Witch lore, folk magic, and general folklore.

Badger

The badger, like the ferret and the snake, is a creature of the earth—one that penetrates the mysteries of the Underworld. The badger symbolizes courage in the face of adversity and the tenacity to see oneself through to the goal despite the obstacles or negative odds. According to oral tradition, during the time of the Inquisition, Witches used the badger as a symbol of perseverance.

The European badger is primarily nocturnal, appearing from its burrow around dusk. The badger as a night creature readily associates it with Witchcraft. A few English Witch trial transcripts mention Familiars in the form of badgers.

Bat

The bat is a creature of the night, much like the Witch. It symbolizes the power to navigate in darkness, and thereby represents the student of the occult arts. The bat is the only mammal capable of actual flight in the manner of a bird. During the classical period bats were symbols of vigilance. Sentries were known to drink potions made from the eyes of bats in a belief that this prevented a person from falling asleep.

In the early bestiaries of medieval times the bat was a symbol of unity, drawn from the fact that bats cluster together in caves. By the eleventh century A.D., popular opinion concerning the bat assigned an evil nature to it. As the Church continued to equate everything associated with paganism as evil the bat entered the ranks of the agents of the Christian devil.

In ancient Europe the bat was related to dragon symbolism because it was winged and lived in a cave. The bat was also a symbol of death and the Underworld. Woodcuts appearing in the Middle Ages and Renaissance periods depict demons as well as Satan himself wearing bat wings. In European folklore Witches were believed to be able to transform into bats. The blood of a bat smeared on a broom was thought to impart the power of flight to a Witch.

Cat

The cat has been revered for thousands of years, and was associated with the Egyptian goddesses Isis and Bast. The black cat in particular was sacred to deities of the night sky and the Underworld. In ancient myths it was believed that certain goddesses were able to take on the outer form of a cat. The ancient writers Ovid, Lucian, and the mythographer Antoninus Liberalis all mention that the moon goddess Diana/Artemis changed into a cat on certain occasions.

In the book the *Cult of the Cat* by Patricia Dale-Green (New York: Weathervane Books, 1963) the author writes of the cat: "Like the moon it comes to life at night, escaping from humanity and wandering over the house tops with its eyes beaming out through the darkness." The ability of the cat's pupil to change from a round to sliver shape associated it with the changing form of the moon from crescent to full. Ancient Roman writers mentioned the eyes of cats and the glowing effect in darkness when torches were present. The cat's eyes glowing in the darkness, as did the moon itself, also served to make the lunar association. The changes in the cat's pupil, likened to the phases of the moon, symbolize the psychic vision of the cat.

Professor Ronald Engels writes, in his book *Classical Cat* (London: Routledge, 1999), of several legends associated with the moon and the cat. Engels recounts the legend in which the moon brought forth the cat, and the cat is therefore the child of the moon. According to Engels, the first literary source in which the cat appears is a play written by Plautus, who lived around 200 B.C.E. However, images of cats appear in art among the Etruscans as early as the sixth century B.C.E. According to Engels, Plautus portrays cats as "despoilers of virgins."

This theme appears also in an old legend about the goddess Diana, and the Roman god Lucifer who was the herald of the sun:

> Diana was the first created before all creation; in her
> were all things; out of herself, the first darkness, she di-
> vided herself; into darkness and light she was divided.
> Lucifer, her brother and her son, herself and her other
> half, was the light.

And when Diana saw the light was so beautiful, the light which was her other half, her brother Lucifer, she yearned for it with exceeding great desire. Wishing to receive the light again into her darkness, to swallow it up in rapture, in delight, she trembled with desire. This desire was the Dawn.

But Lucifer, the light, fled from her, and would not yield to her wishes; he was the light which flies into the most distant parts of heaven, the mouse which flies before the cat.

Then Diana went to the fathers of the Beginning, to the mothers, the spirits who were before the first spirit, and lamented unto them that she could not prevail with Lucifer. And they praised her for her courage; they told her that to rise she must fall; to become the chief of goddesses she must become a mortal.

And in the ages, in the course of time, when the world was made, Diana went on Earth, as did Lucifer, who had fallen, and Diana taught magic, whence came Witches and fairies and goblins—all that is like man yet not mortal.

And it came thus that Diana took the form of a cat. Her brother had a cat whom he loved beyond all creatures, and it slept every night on his bed, a cat beautiful beyond all other creatures, a fairy: he did not know it.

Diana prevailed with the cat to change forms with her; so she lay with her brother, and in the darkness assumed her own form, and so by Lucifer became the mother of Aradia. But when in the morning he found that he lay by his sister, and that light had been conquered by darkness, Lucifer was extremely angry; but Diana sang to him a spell, a song of power, and he was silent, the song of the night which soothes to sleep; he could say nothing. So Diana with her wiles of Witchcraft so charmed him that he yielded to her love. This was the first fascination; she hummed the song, it was as the buzzing of bees, a spinning wheel spinning life. She had such passion for Witchcraft, and became so powerful therein, that her greatness could not be hidden.

And thus it came to pass one night, at the meeting of all the sorceresses and fairies, she declared that she would darken the heavens and turn all the stars into mice.

All those who were present said: "If thou canst do such a strange thing, having risen to such power, thou shalt be our queen."

Diana went into the street; she took the bladder of an ox and a piece of Witch-money, which has an edge like a knife—with such money Witches cut the earth from men's foot-tracks—and she cut the earth, and with it and many mice she filled the bladder, and blew into the bladder till it burst.

And there came a great marvel, for the earth which was in the bladder became the round heaven above, and for three days there was a great rain; the mice became stars or rain. And having made the heaven and the stars and the rain, Diana became Queen of the Witches; she was the cat who ruled the star-mice, the heaven and the rain.*

Norse legend tells of Freya, goddess of love and fertility, whose chariot was pulled by two black cats. Some versions of the tale claim they became swift black horses, possessed by the Devil. After serving Freya for seven years, the cats were rewarded by being turned into Witches, disguised as black cats. Traits associated with cats include cleverness, unpredictability, healing, and Witchcraft, since in ancient times it was believed that Witches took the form of their cats at night.

---

* Charles Godfrey Leland, *Aradia; Gospel of the Witches*. London: David Nutt, 1899.

Friday has long been associated with Freya as her sacred day. During the Middle Ages the Church sanctioned the burning of live cats on Good Friday and other "holy days" in the belief that cats were devils. Some commentators believe that the departed spirits of these cats became Familiars for local Witches. It was largely in the Middle Ages that the black cat became affiliated with evil. Because cats are nocturnal and roam at night, they were believed to be supernatural servants of Witches, or even Witches themselves.

Dragons

Dragons are associated with guardianship much like the gargoyle, and they protect hidden treasures. Dragons also appear in many fairytales associated with young maidens. Such popular folktales also include Witches and figures like Rapunsel and Snow White. In modern tales dragons often possess magical powers and are associated with the sorcerer or sorceress.

One of the most ancient accounts to mention a Witch and a dragon appears in the Greek tales of the hero Jason and the Witch known as Medea. Medea aided Jason with her magic when he journeyed to obtain the magical golden fleece, which was guarded by a dragon.

In this Greek tale, and another featuring Cadmus of Tyre, when the dragon is slain a voice speaks from within it, directing the hero to plant the teeth of the dragon in the soil. The voice promises a reward for this action, but instead the buried teeth sprout an army of avenging warriors.

Ferret

The ferret is a creature of the earth, an animal that penetrates the mysteries of the Underworld. Witch trials, particularly in England, make mention of the ferret as a familiar spirit kept by witches. The case of Mother Waterhouse is one example, and other Essex witches confessed to possessing ferrets as their Familiars. In 1582 a witch known as Mother Bennet was said to possess a spirit that looked much like a ferret. The trial of Joan Prentice in 1589 features a talking ferret named Bidd.

According to old lore, the ferret symbolizes an inquisitive nature, especially regarding hidden objects, and is attributed with the ability to move about in silence. This is one of the reasons why the ferret was associated with the mysteries of Witchcraft. Here the ferret represents the occult seeker in relentless search of the inner secrets.

Frog

The frog is a creature of transformation, symbolized by the tadpole to frog stage of development. Frogs are creatures that live in both land and water environments. This symbolizes the "dweller in both worlds" concept.

The frog appears in post-Paleolithic prehistory in iconography suggestive of the uterus. In European folklore the frog is often associated with themes of pregnancy. Some anthropologists such as Marija Gimbutas link the frog/toad to the "wandering womb" figure noted in ancient Egyptian sources. Images of "frog women" and anthropromorphized frogs with human features appear around 10,000 B.C.E. Frogs depicted with human vulva appear around 6300 B.C.E. Concerning this theme, it is interesting to note that a votive tablet to the Madonna dated 1811 depicts her accompanied by a frog with an exposed human vulva. The tablet originated in the Alpine region of Bavaria, and a copy appears in chapter 23 of *The Language of the Goddess* by Marija Gimbutas.

In German lore the Frog Goddess Holla/Holle inhabits bogs, ponds, wells, and caves. Holla/Holle is also associated with the red apple, a symbol of life. The Egyptian goddess Haquit (the

Creatrix) appears with the head of a frog, which was also her hieroglyphic symbol. The Greek goddess Hecate was ascribed the epithet of *Baubo*, which means "toad."

Frogs are "listeners" of things heard in the darkness, and can reveal many secrets to the Witch. According to oral tradition it is a very old technique to use the croaking of frogs to induce a mental state of trance. In such a state questions can be asked and answered.

Gargoyles

Gargoyles are creatures associated with guardianship and protection. The gargoyle figure often stood over the entrance to sacred or important structures, and is often found in the supporting columns of cathedrals. The most common gargoyle image is the Florentine style, bearing bat-like wings. Their faces are usually those of a dog, lion, wolf, or an imp. The Tuscan gargoyle has a face like a bulldog and wings more like those of a dragon. He also has a chain around his neck. The Gothic gargoyle dates from a slightly later period and is commonly seen in the British Isles. It has a variety of face styles including humanoid, and is more somber in appearance, often resembling the Christian stereotype of a demon.

The association of the gargoyle with the Witch arises from occultism in general, and is not rooted in the distant past. Since the Church chose to assign anything Pagan to an evil or demonic nature, the Witch and the Gargoyle shared a common nature in the minds of an unenlightened era.

Goblin

The term *Goblin* is derived from the name Gob, who was king of the dwarves or gnomes. A goblin is, therefore, literally one of Gob's followers. In common folklore, following the rise of Christianity, the goblin appears as an ugly and mischievous spirit or sprite. It is strongly identified with Puck or Robin Goodfellow. The word hobgoblin is a variant of the title Rob-goblin or Robin goblin.

The following is an old tale regarding a goblin and the deities of associated with classical and medieval Witchcraft:

> Many centuries ago there was a goblin, or spirit or devil-angel, and Mercury, who was the god of speed and of quickness, being much pleased with this imp, bestowed on him the gift of running like the wind, with the privilege that whatever he pursued, be it spirit, a human being, or animal, he should certainly overtake or catch it.
>
> This goblin had a beautiful sister, who like him, ran errands, not for the gods, but for the goddesses (there was a female god for every male, even down to the small spirits); and Diana on the same day gave to this fairy the power that, whoever might chase her, she should, if pursued, never be overtaken.
>
> One day the brother saw his sister speeding like a flash of lightning across the heaven, and he felt a sudden strange desire in rivalry to overtake her. So he dashed after as she flitted on; but though it was his destiny to catch her, she had been fated never to be caught, and so the will of one supreme god was balanced by that of another.
>
> So the two kept flying round and round the edge of heaven, and at first all the gods roared with laughter, but when they understood the case, they grew serious, and asked one another how it was to end. Then the great father-god said, "Behold the earth, which is in darkness and gloom! I will change the sister into a Moon, and her brother into a sun. And so shall she ever escape him, yet will he ever catch her with his light, which shall fall on her from afar; for the rays of the sun are his hands, which reach forth with burning grasp, yet which are ever eluded.

And thus it is said that this race begins anew with the first of every month, when the moon, being cold, is covered with as many coats as an onion. But while the race is being run, as the moon becomes warm she casts off one garment after another, till she is naked and then stops, and then when dressed the race begins again.*

Hare

Hares were strongly associated with Witches. The writings of Giraldus Cambrensis in the twelfth century reveal the belief that a witch can transform into a hare is a very "old belief." In 1662 Isobel Gowdie of Auldarne confessed that she and other members of her coven transformed themselves at will by saying three times:

> I shall go into a hare,
> with sorrow and sych and meikle care;
> And I shall go in the Devil's name
> Ay while I come home again.

When they wished to resume human form they said,

> Hare, hare, God send thee care.
> I am in a hare's likeness just now,
> But I shall be in a woman's likeness even now.**

A Witch trial in Trent was focused upon a girl who claimed to have inherited a "witch's thong" from her grandmother. Whenever she tied the thong around herself she would turn into a hare. In this form she often heckled a local forester who lived in the vicinity.

Since Pagan times the hare was revered as a sacred creature associated with fertility and spring. In northern Europe the hare

---

* Ibid.
** www.museumofwitchcraft.com/mow/mow/hare.html.

was sacred to the spring goddess Eostre or Ostara. The Christian festival known as Easter bears a form of her name, and the custom of the "Easter Bunny" is associated with this time.

In pre-Christian European Paganism the hare was associated with the goddess of the moon. The hare was also associated with the spring equinox and the autumn equinox. In this connection the hare symbolized the new life of spring and the decline of life into death and renewal. According to an oral tradition among witches, hares sleep in nest-like formations that strongly resemble the ground nests of lapwing birds. Reportedly some confusion arose between the two, leading some people to believe that hares laid eggs or in some way were connected to the appearance of eggs. There is some suggestion that the figure of the Easter Bunny and Easter eggs arises from this old folk belief.

Imps

The imp is one of the most classic creatures associated with Witches since the Middle Ages. In occult lore the imp is a spirit being, a conscious entity belonging to the class of nature spirits. The name imp derives from the Medieval Latin *impotus*, which means to graft. In Old English the root word was *impa*, which referred to a young sprout. The Greek root of the word was *emphuein*, which means to implant (*phuein* means to make grow). In olden days the term imp was also applied to the grafting of new wing feathers on trained falcons and hawks. The Church viewed the imp as a servant of the devil, relegating it to the category of minor demons.

Villagers of the English town of Canewdon often told stories of the local Witch, George Pickingill. According to the villagers, Pickingill would sit idly smoking his pipe while a crew of imps worked his land for him.

Mouse

In old legends Witches were believed to be able to transform into mice. Some tales include the belief that the soul of a Witch appears as a mouse. Margaret Wyard, an accused Witch of Bury St. Edmonds in Suffolk, England, confessed to having mice among her familiars. Other Witches in the area admitted to having two "heavy and hairy" mice as familiars. In 1662, the young daughters of Samuel Pacy captured "invisible mice," which they threw on a fire. One mouse "screeched like a rat" and the other "flash'd like to Gun-Powder."

A sixteenth-century trial records the confession of a woman in Essex who claimed to have three mouse-shaped imps named Daynty, Prettyman, and Littleman. Another woman had four, named Sparrow, Robyn, James, and Prickeare. In the seventeenth-century trial of Ann Armstrong (a Northumbrian Witch), she confessed that after betraying a member of her coven she was forced to sing while they danced around her in a variety of physical forms. First they took on the shape of a hare, returned to their own shape, and then appeared again in cat form, while some took the form of a mouse.

Owl

The owl has been associated with Witchcraft since the classical era. The screech owl in particular has a long history in the tales of Witchcraft. The Latin term for a screech owl was the word *strigis*, from which is derived *striga* and *strix*. The latter names were used to refer to Witches.

The sound of an owl at night, its silent flight, and its form backlighted by the full moon gave rise to occult legends regarding the owl. The ability to see in the dark became a metaphor for the oracle and divinatory powers of the Witch. Here the owl, as

a symbol of wisdom, joined with the Witch as a person of visionary powers.

Raven

Legends connected to Witchcraft from the fifteenth to the eigh-
teenth centuries portray Witches flying up chimneys at night, on
their way to the Sabbat, in the form of a raven, crow, feathered
toad, black cat, or a male goat. Superstitious villagers believed
that ravens and crows spied for the witch during the day, report-
ing back at night.

The raven is a messenger of the gods, and a teacher-spirit that
brings revelation through the creation of conflict. The blackness
of the raven's feathers has caused this bird to be associated with
the night and the Underworld. Also, because it is a scavenger,
often feeding on dead animals, the raven has been associated
with death.

The raven as a messenger makes an excellent Familiar image
and can be used as a carrier of magic across distances. The black
color aids in night travel, making it difficult to detect. The raven is
one of the few scavengers who will also perform as a bird of prey.

Snake

The snake, like the ferret, is a creature of the earth and one that
penetrates the mysteries of the Underworld. According to a
Basque tradition there exists a secret Witches' realm beneath the
earth "where all things abound, especially milk and honey, which
run in abundant rivers."

Snakes are intimately connected with Witchcraft and goddesses of Witchcraft. The ancient Roman Horace associates the
Roman goddess Proserpina with the worship of Witches. Proserpina is the goddess of night and the Underworld. Her name is

derived from the Latin *serpere*, to creep or crawl, rendered *proser-pere*, meaning to crawl forward. She was identified with the moon and the serpent because both disappear into the earth and seemingly change shape in their overall movement. The Italian Witch charm known as the cimaruta bears an image of the serpent moving along the edge of a crescent moon. Like Hecate, the serpent, torch, and key are all symbols associated with Proserpina.

The snake is a symbol of transformation, symbolized by the ability to shed its skin as it grows. The ability of the snake to coil its body reflects the ancient symbol of the spiral, a design appearing in Neolithic tomb art.

Spider

The ability of spiders to spin webs has caused them to be associated with magic in many folklore legends throughout Europe. Some commentators have likened the process to casting spells, and terms like "the thread of magic" and "a web of magic" indicate such beliefs.

Spinning and weaving have long been associated with the Fates. Professor Eva Pocs (*Between the Living and the Dead*, Central European University Press, 1999) states there are thirty-six documented cases, spanning three centuries of Witch trials, in which a "fate goddess" appears in Hungarian Witchcraft. Poc also states that all the goddesses mentioned in Witchcraft trials are associated with spinning. She notes that Hungarian Witch trials mention Witches spinning, weaving, or carrying spindles.

Supernatural Familiars

Some creatures associated with Witchcraft fall into the category of "supernatural" beings. The association to Witchcraft of imps and goblins in the form of the succubus and incubus appears first documented around the end of the seventh century. The association of gargoyles and dragons with Witches came relatively late in the Middle Ages and was most likely an addition to themes that met the agenda of the Church. In popular lore and fairytales the Witch appears in both old and new settings and associations.

Toad

The toad, like the frog, is a creature of transformation, likewise symbolized by the tadpole-to-toad stages of development. Unlike the frog however, the toad is essentially a creature of the land. This symbolizes the "crosser of the threshold" concept.

The toad was sacred to Hecate, and to Ragana, the Lithuanian goddess of death and regeneration. In some folk traditions toads were dressed in velvet and given bells to decorate their legs. The horn-like area on the toad's head links it to pagan elements, and Witches reportedly used toad's spittle in their ointments. It is known that some toads produce a chemical secretion that can induce euphoria or hallucinations.

Old writings concerning the toad mention that witches used the toad to call up the spirits of the dead. Toads were believed to have a stone inside their head called the toad stone. According to occult legend this stone possessed both medical and magical properties. A mysterious sect known as the Toadmen were well-known in England, and were said to possess power over horses. Their power was received through a ritual that involved obtaining a key-shaped bone from the toad's body. Frogs were also said to have a key-like bone.

Witch trials in Sweden record that during the Sabbats little Witch children played at being shepherds over their flocks of toads. In the records of Spanish Witchcraft trials (circa 1610) the toad also appears. In one trial the accused was said to bear a toad-like mark stamped on his eyelid. He confessed to possessing a toad with the power to make him invisible and to transport him to distant places. It also allowed the Witch to take on the form of various animals.

The ancient Persians associated the toad with Ahriman, and depicted his attendants as toads. In the Tyrol region toads were once believed to be the souls of sinners undergoing penance. In the Middle Ages a belief arose that toads were people who made pilgrimage vows, but died before being able to fulfill them.

APPENDIX 3

NAMES OF FAMILIARS

The names of Familiar spirits appearing here have been drawn from Witchcraft trial transcripts. I have included them simply for historical interest and folklore curiosity.

Abrahel	Greednut
Ball	Griffart
Bara	Grimalkin
Barrabarri	Grissel Greedigut
Berit	Guli
Bidd	Guillaume
Blackman	Hammerlein
Borrel	Haussibut
Brunet	Hiff Hiff
Dandy	Hinkebein
Daynty	Holt
Farmara	Ilemanzar
Federwisch	Jacke
Galifas	Jamara
Gill	James
Ginifert	Jezebel

Juson
Krutli
Littleman
Lizabet
Lucifel
Maitre
Mermet
Newes
Oberycom
Parsley
Pecke-in-the-Crown
Piggin
Prettyman
Prickeare
Puss
Pyewackett
Ragot
Raphas

Revel
Robbin
Robinet
Robert
Robin Artisson
Rutterkin
Sacke & Sugar
Sathan
Sparrow
Suckin
Tartas
Tibb
Tiffin
Tissy
Titty
Verd-Joli
Verdelet
Vinegar Tom

APPENDIX 4

THE WITCHES' ALPHABET

A	⁊	J	℧	S	⅋
B	⅊	K	ℭ	T	⁊
C	⁊	L	⅋	U	⅌
D	⁊	M	⅋	V	⅌
E	⁊	N	℔	W	⅌
F	⅊	O	ℳ	X	℧
G	℧	P	⅊	Y	⅋
H	⅋	Q	⅊	Z	℔
I	℧	R	ℳ		

151

BIBLIOGRAPHY

Alexander, Hartley Burr. *The World's Rim: Great Mysteries of the North American Indians*. Lincoln, Nebr.: Univ. of Nebraska Press, 1967.

Andrews, Ted. *Animal-Speak: The Spiritual and Magical Powers of Creatures Great and Small*. St. Paul: Llewellyn Publications, 1993.

____. *Animal Wise: The Spirit Language and Signs of Nature*. Jackson: Dragonhawk Publishing, 1999.

Ankarloo, Bengt, and Clark Stuart (editors). *Witchcraft and Magic in Europe: Biblical and Pagan Societies*. Philadelphia: University of Pennsylvania Press, 2001.

Baker, Margaret. *Discovering the Folklore of Plants*. Princes Risborough: Shire Publications Ltd., 1999.

Biedermann, Hans. *Dictionary of Symbolism: Cultural Icons and the Meanings Behind Them*. New York: Facts on File, 1989.

Curran, Bob. *The Creatures of Celtic Myth*. London: Cassell & Co., 2000.

Dale-Green, Patricia. *The Cult of the Cat*. New York: Weathervane Books, 1963.

Devlin, Judith. *The Superstitious Mind: French Peasants and the Supernatural in the Nineteenth Century*. New Haven and London: Yale University Press. 1987.

Engles, Donald. *Classical Cats*. London: Routledge, 1999.

Evans-Wentz, W. Y. *The Fairy Faith in Celtic Countries*. New York: Citadel Press, 1994.

Fortune, Dion. *Aspects of Occultism*. Wellingborough: Aquarian Press, 1973.

Green, Miranda. *Animals in Celtic Life and Myth*. London: Routledge, 1992.

Hazlitt, W. C. *Dictionary of Faiths & Folklore: Beliefs, Superstitions and Popular Customs*. London: Bracken Books, 1995.

Howey, M. OldField. *The Cat in Magic, Mythology, and Religion*. New York: Crescent Books, 1989.

Lavendar, Susan, and Anna Franklin. *Herb Craft: A Guide to the Shamanic and Ritual Use of Herbs*. London: Capall Bann, 1996.

Lindahl, Carl, John. McNamara, and John Lindow (editors). *Medieval Folklore: A Guide to Myths, Legends, Tales, Beliefs, and Customs*. Oxford: Oxford University Press, 2000.

Phipson, Emma. *The Animal-Lore of Shakespeare's Time*. London: Kegan Paul, Trench & Co., 1983.

Pickering, David. *Dictionary of Witchcraft*. London: Cassell Book, 1996.

Roderick, Timothy. *The Once Unknown Familiar*. St. Paul: Llewellyn Publications, 1994.

Simpson, J., and S. Roud. *Oxford Dictionary of English Folklore*. Oxford: Oxford University Press, 2000.

Spence, Lewis. *An Encyclopedia of Occultism*. New York: University Books, 1960.

____. *The Fairy Faith in Britain*. Kila: Kessinger Publishing Company, 2000.

Vickery, Roy. *Oxford Dictionary of Plant-Lore*. Oxford: N.p., 1995.

Walker, Charles. *The Encyclopedia of the Occult*. New York: Crescent Books, 1995.

Index

TO WRITE TO THE AUTHOR

If you wish to contact the author or would like more information about this book, please write to the author in care of Llewellyn Worldwide and we will forward your request. Both the author and publisher appreciate hearing from you and learning of your enjoyment of this book and how it has helped you. Llewellyn Worldwide cannot guarantee that every letter written to the author can be answered, but all will be forwarded. Write to:

Raven Grimassi

C/o Llewellyn Worldwide

P.O. Box 64383, Dept. 0-7387-0339-7

St. Paul, MN 55164-0383, U.S.A.

Please enclose a self-addressed stamped envelope for reply, or $1.00 to cover costs. If outside U.S.A., enclose international postal reply coupon.

Many of Llewellyn's authors have websites with additional information and resources. For more information, please visit our website at http://www.llewellyn.com.

Encyclopedia of Wicca & Witchcraft

Raven Grimassi

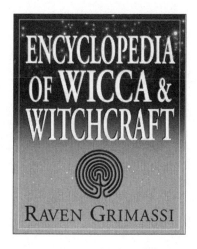

This indispensable reference work provides both a historical and cultural foundation for modern Wicca and Witchcraft, and it is the first to be written by an actual practitioner of the Craft.

Other encyclopedias present a series of surface topics such as tools, sabbats, Witchcraft trials, and various mundane elements. Unique to this encyclopedia is its presentation of Wicca/Witchcraft as a spiritual path, connecting religious concepts and spirituality to a historical background and a modern system of practice. It avoids the inclusion of peripheral entries typically included, and deals only with Wicca/Witchcraft topics, old and new, traditional and eclectic. It also features modern Wiccan expressions, sayings, and terminology. Finally, you will find a storehouse of information on European folklore and Western Occultism as related to modern Wicca/Witchcraft.

1-56718-257-7, 528 pp., 8 x 10,
300+ illus. & photos $24.95

Hereditary Witchcraft
Secrets of the Old Religion
Raven Grimassi

This book is about the Old Religion of Italy, and contains material that is at least 100 years old, much of which has never before been seen in print. This overview of the history and lore of the Hereditary Craft will show you how the Italian witches viewed nature, magick, and the occult forces. Nothing in this book is mixed with, or drawn from, any other Wiccan traditions.

The Italian witches would gather beneath the full moon to worship a goddess (Diana) and a god (Dianus). The roots of Italian Witchcraft extend back into the prehistory of Italy, in the indigenous Mediterranean/Aegean neolithic cult of the Great Goddess. Follow its development to the time of the Inquisition, when it had to go into hiding to survive, and to the present day. Uncover surprising discoveries of how expressions of Italian Witchcraft have been taught and used in this century.

1-56718-256-9, 288 pp., 7½ x 9⅛, 31 illus.   **$14.95**

Italian Witchcraft

The Old Religion of Southern Europe

(Formerly titled *Ways of the Strega*,
now revised and expanded)

Raven Grimassi

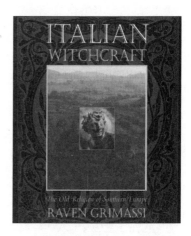

Discover the rich legacy of magick and ritual handed down by
Italian witches through the gen-
erations. Trace the roots of the Italian Pagan tradition as it sur-
vives the times, confronted by Christianity, revived in the 14th
century by the Holy Strega, and passed on as the Legend of Aradia to the present day. Explore the secrets of Janarra (lunar)
witches, Tanarra (star) witches, and Fanarra (ley lines) witches.
Their ancient wisdoms come together in the modern Aridian
tradition, presented here for both theoretical understanding and
everyday practice. You will learn the gospel of Aradia, and the
powerful practice of "casting shadows," an ancient tradition only
now available to the public. *Italian Witchcraft* also gives you the
practical how-tos of modern Strega traditions, including making
tools, casting and breaking spells, seasonal and community rites,
honoring the Watchers, creating a Spirit Flame, and much more.

1-56718-259-3, 336 pp., 7½ x 9⅛, illus. $14.95

Wiccan Magick
Inner Teachings of the Craft
Raven Grimassi

Wiccan Magick is a serious and complete study for those who desire to understand the inner meanings, techniques, and symbolism of magick as an occult art. Magick within modern Wicca is an eclectic blending of many occult traditions that evolved from the ancient beliefs and practices in both Europe, the Middle East, and Asia. *Wiccan Magick* covers the full range of magickal and ritual practices as they pertain to both modern ceremonial and shamanic Wicca.

Come to understand the evolution of the Craft, the ancient magickal current that flows from the past to the present, and the various aspects included in ritual, spell casting, and general theology. When you understand why something exists within a ritual structure, you will know better how to build upon the underlying concepts to create ritual that is meaningful to you.

1-56718-255-0, 240 pp., 6 x 9 $12.95

The Wiccan Mysteries
Ancient Origins & Teachings
Raven Grimassi

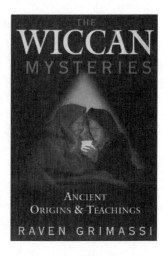

What you will encounter in *The Wiccan Mysteries* is material that was once taught only in the initiate levels of the old Wiccan Mystery Traditions, and to which many solitary practitioners have never had access. Learn the inner meanings of Wiccan rites, beliefs, and practices, and discover the time-proven concepts that created, maintained, and carried Wiccan beliefs up into this modern era. In reflecting back upon the wisdom of our ancestors, neo-Wiccans can draw even greater sustenance from the spiritual stores of Wicca—the Old Religion.

The Wiccan Mysteries will challenge you to expand your understanding and even reexamine your own perceptions. Wicca is essentially a Celtic-oriented religion, but its Mystery Tradition is derived from several outside cultures as well. You will come away with a sense of the rich heritage that was passed from one human community to another, and that now resides within this system for spiritual development.

1-56718-254-2, 312 pp., 6 x 9 $14.95

The Witches' Craft

The Roots of Witchcraft &
Magical Transformation

Raven Grimassi

Enter the old forms of Witch-craft (many of which have been forgotten), and learn the ways and techniques that provide a solid foundation for further study, qualifying you to become the local village Witch! The ma-terial is selected for its authenticity, and demonstrates that Witchcraft is an evolving religion, not a modern construction.

Containing many aspects of Witchcraft never before seen in print, these pages will take you through the labyrinth of Witch-craft's history and deliver up the secrets of the Witches' craft, which lie deep within the center of the maze. It is a treasure wor-thy of pursuit.

In *The Witches' Craft* you will find a serious and in-depth study of the old ways of Witchcraft. This is the first book to present the entire unedited method of constructing the witches' ladder, and it preserves much of what has been forgotten, misplaced, or dis-carded through the years. The book also contains correspondence between the author and Doreen Valiente that sheds further light on the evolution of Witchcraft as it is practiced today.

0-7387-0265-X, 312 pp., 7½ x 9⅛ $16.95

To Order, Call 1-877 NEW WRLD
Prices subject to change without notice

Is Your Pet Psychic?

Developing Psychic Communication with Your Pet

Richard Webster

Cats that can redict earthquakes, dogs that improve marriages, and horses that can add and subtract—animals have long been known to possess these aznd other amazing talents. Now you can experience for yourself the innate psychic abilities of your pet with *Is Your Pet Psychic.*

Learn to exchange ideas with your pet that will enhance your relationship in many ways. Transmit and receive thoughts when you're at a distance, help lost pets find their way home, even communicate with pets who are deceased.

Whether your animal walks, flies, or swims, it is possible to establish a psychic bond and a more meaningful relationship. This book is full of instructions, as well as true case studies from past and present.

0-7387-0193-9, 288 pp., 5³⁄₁₆ x 8 $12.95

Psychic Pets & Spirit Animals

True Stories from the Files of FATE magazine

FATE Magazine Editorial Staff

In spite of all our scientific knowledge about animals, important questions remain about the nature of animal intelligence. Now, a large body of personal testimony compels us to raise still deeper questions. Are some animals, like some people, psychic? If human beings survive death, do animals? Do bonds exist between people and animals that are beyond our ability to comprehend?

Psychic Pets & Spirit Animals is a varied collection from the past fifty years of the real-life experiences of ordinary people with creatures great and small. You will encounter psychic pets, ghost animals, animal omens, extraordinary human-animal bonds, pet survival after death, phantom protectors, and the weird creatures of cryptozoology. Dogs, cats, birds, horses, wolves, grizzly bears—even insects—are the heroes of shockingly true reports that illustrate just how little we know about the animals we think we know best.

The true stories in *Psychic Pets & Spirit Animals* suggest that animals are, in many ways, more like us than we think—and that they, too, can step into the strange and unknowable realm of the paranormal, where all things are possible.

1-56718-299-2, 272 pp., mass market   **$4.99**